LEGENDARY YACHTS

America rerigged with straight masts in the 1890s

BILL ROBINSON

LEGENDARY YACHTS

DAVID McKAY COMPANY, INC.
NEW YORK

Also by Bill Robinson

The Science of Sailing
New Boat
A Berth to Bermuda
Where the Trade Winds Blow
Expert Sailing
Over the Horizon
The World of Yachting
Better Sailing for Boys and Girls
The Best from Yachting (editor)
The America's Cup Races (coauthor)
The Sailing Life
The Right Boat for You
America's Sailing Book
A Sailor's Tales

Library of Congress Catalog Card Number: 70-158165

1 2 3 4 5 6 7 8 9

Manufactured in the United States of America

Contents

Preface   *vii*

PART I GRAND BEGINNINGS

1 *It Started with Royalty*   *1*

2 *Cleopatra's Barge*   *17*

3 *America*   *29*

4 *The Vanderbilts*   *47*

5 *The Morgans*   *67*

PART II THE GOLDEN AGE

6 *The Height of Luxury*   *89*

7 *Aloha*   *113*

8 *Sea Cloud*   *127*

9 *Atlantic*   *137*

10 *Savarona*   *151*

11 *Ranger*   *161*

PART III A CHANGE OF EMPHASIS

12 *After World War II*   *175*

13 *Nina*   *193*

14 *Ticonderoga*   *209*

15 *Finisterre*   *229*

16 *Chanticleer*   *245*

17 *Intrepid*   *257*

18 *Courageous*   *291*

Index   *307*

Acknowledgments

Grateful acknowledgment is made to Mr. Sohei Hohri, librarian of the New York Yacht Club, for his help in assembling many of the pictures from the archives of the library. The author is especially indebted to *Yachting* magazine for the use of its inventory file. Thanks also go to Stanley Rosenfeld for providing many of the pictures from the files of his studio, most of them taken by his father, the late Morris Rosenfeld, and to John Mecray for his painting of *Courageous* that appears on the jacket.

Bahamas Ministry of Tourism, pp. 177, 228, 241
Barlow, Peter, p. 256
Barker, B. D., p. 262 top
Beckner Photo Service, p. 224
Beken & Son, p. 43
Bermuda News Bureau, pp. 206, 234, 235 top
Cattanch, Alex J., p. 85
Evinrude, Ralph, pp. 244, 249, 250, 251, 254
Hopf, John T., pp. 269, 272
Jamaica Tourist Board, pp. 213, 214
Mariners Museum, Newport News, Va., pp. 95 top, 93 top
Moore, R. R., pp. 78–79

Moss, Frank, p. 191
Nakajima, Fusanori, p. 201
Newmark, Esther, p. 183
Peabody Museum—G. Crowninshield, p. 19
Rimington, Critchell, p. 126
Robinson, Bill, pp. 180–181, 190, 192, 219, 261, 267, 270, 274, 275, 278, 279, 284, 288, 293, 296, 300, 304, 306
Rosenfeld, Morris, pp. 50, 51, 54, 58, 61, 81–82, 88, 91, 104 bottom, 111, 115, 133 bottom, 143, 153, 156, 157, 158, 159, 160, 163, 167, 170 bottom, 174, 186, 187 top, 195, 202, 208, 233, 235 bottom, 242, 266, 268, 290

Preface

These are the great yachts

Not that they are the only ones. Over the years, there have been many graceful, lovely yachts, in sail and power, some as large as ocean liners, some not so big but impressive for other reasons and by other standards. They have made an appearance on the scene and been admired, but then have been forgotten when they went to the ship-breakers or became banana boats in some Caribbean backwater.

Only certain vessels have left a reputation or an influence beyond the span of their peak years. These are the ones that are still remembered when yachtsmen gather, whether for their special grace, their astounding size and lavishness, or for outstanding feats that they have performed. With some, it was a famous name carried on for several vessels. Others bore a name that will forever mean that one, even though others might have used it, inadvertently or on purpose.

This has to be an arbitrary selection, mostly American in its emphasis, and even this will bring arguments for boats that have had a regional influence, or affected a certain group or type. All these yachts have meant more and have left a permanent mark. That is all they have in common, and this is their story.

Part I

GRAND BEGINNINGS

The first royal yacht made the steam yacht respectable

1

It Started with Royalty

It had to start with royalty. The pomp and circumstance, the aura of regal splendor that surrounded yachting in the era of the great yachts, and the later traditions they fostered, could only have been inspired by royal example. Cleopatra, of course, had her barge, Charles II is traditionally credited with owning the first real yacht, the *Mary*, in 1660, and Queen Elizabeth I had preceded him with a small sailing vessel oddly called *Rat of Wight*, but they had no ordinary yachtsmen to inspire.

Not until 1817, when the Prince Regent ordered sent to the newly formed organization known as the Yacht Club at Cowes, England, a note saying "you are to consider this an official notice of His Royal Highness's desire" to become a member, were the prerogatives of royalty joined with the pretensions of lesser mortals in the pursuit of pleasure afloat. The club promptly raised its dues, doubled the size of the requirement for membership to a minimum of a 20-ton yacht, and changed its name to Royal Yacht Club. Later to become known as the Royal Yacht Squadron, also at the request of the Regent, the first yacht club to come down to modern times in a direct line of operation thereby acquired the trappings of royalty, and they became a traditional part of the sport.

It took some time for the yachts themselves to acquire much distinction, and two souls, who certainly can be called rugged in their individuality, had much to do with this. They were a peppery gentleman known as Thomas Assheton-Smith and Queen Victoria. The early yachts were little more than floating houseboats, rigged only for sail, and one candidate for membership in the Squadron was supposedly blackballed because his vessel had taken two months to sail from London to Cowes and also had brick bulkheads in the cabin. Mr. Assheton-Smith, who had built five sailing yachts in the early days of the Squadron, and whose cutter *Elizabeth* took part in the club's first race (and lost through a dismasting), tired of sailing vessels and, in 1829, decided to go to steam. He tried to get approval for a steam yacht, was turned down and even accused of possible commercialism in building one, and as Peter Heaton reports in his *Yachting, A History,* "withdrew his name from the club." His first steamer was *Menai,* of 400 tons, costing £20,000, and he went on to build seven more as a real pioneer of the genre.

He remained an unfashionable pioneer, however, with the anti-pollution forces of the day decrying the "murky vomitings of the furnaces," until Queen Victoria was won over to the convenience of a power-driven vessel. The Regent, who became George IV, had been using a ship-rigged yacht called *Royal George* for his lavish entertaining, but the plush vessel was not to Victoria's liking, especially when she often saw steamers passing the becalmed or tide-bound sailing yacht. A woman known for getting her own way, to put it mildly, she had the *Victoria and Albert,* a 200-foot steamer, commissioned in 1843 and promptly set off cruising, visiting such friends and relations as King Louis Philippe of France and King Leopold of Belgium.

It was the second *Victoria and Albert,* however, in 1855, that did much to influence yachtsmen who followed in the Queen's wake. She was 300 feet long, 2,342 tons, a handsome, able paddle-steamer with two stacks. Her interior was designed by Prince Albert personally in a motif of white with gold relief and a chintz wallpaper with moss rosebuds on a white background. In an era in which yachting flourished, along with the heyday of Empire and the free-swinging aftermath of the Industrial Revolution, she was the domi-

The third *Victoria and Albert* at sea

The *V and A* was luxurious but not a good sea boat

nant vessel, a familiar sight at yachting and naval spectacles (and a vindication for Mr. Assheton-Smith).

Sailing yachts became mere racing machines, and the desire to emulate the royal way of life burst forth in a series of steam yachts ever more magnificent and regal. And Americans, stripped of the traditions and trappings of royalty at home, perhaps even tried to outdo the less impressionable British and Europeans in the splendor of their new yachts.

An empire builder, American style, was one of the first to start the tradition. Cornelius Vanderbilt, who delighted in the unofficial title of Commodore, built the first big American steam yacht, *North Star*, and in 1853 dramatized the tradition of the "grand tour" of European harbors with an epic voyage, epic in the scope of its undertaking in those days. Years before him, George Crowninshield of Salem, Mass., had used the fruits of a pre-Industrial Revolution fortune to take a "grand tour" of Europe in 1817 in *Cleopatra's Barge*, popularly called America's first yacht. This sailing vessel was well ahead of her time, and in spirit she was a forerunner of the steam-yacht days.

Commodore Vanderbilt was not to be left alone in his glory for long. Once the distraction of the War Between the States was left behind, the way was clear for a wide-open race for prestige and glory as millionaires vied with each other to produce the most luxurious and fastest yachts. Speed was as important as luxury, especially for New Yorkers when they headed down Long Island Sound for Newport, R.I. Many a yacht went up for sale quickly when she suffered the indignity of having a faster vessel come up astern and pass her on the way to the fashionable watering spot. Mortification was rampant on the fantail of a yacht when an owner had to face his guests as a rival vessel surged on by, leaving a gritty trail of smoke for those on the slower boat to inhale.

At first, the steam yachts of the second half of the nineteenth century were merely sailing yachts with steam added. They had the low, rakish hulls of the schooners popular at the time, clipper bows and several masts that were rigged for sailing, though seldom used. An English adventurer, Sir Thomas Brassey, did conduct a circumnavigation in the brigantine *Sunbeam*, making long passages under sail

Lord Brassey was one of the first yachtsmen to circumnavigate. *Sunbeam* sailed more than she used power.

and using her steam engine for moving through calms and in and out of harbors and rivers.

A yachting historian of the day, Edward S. Jaffray, belittled the *Sunbeam*, however, by pointing out that her best speed under steam was only about 8 knots. She would, he said, "cut but a poor figure in a run up the Hudson or the Sound in company with our better class of yachts." He went on to say that "Every man who gives an order for a steam yacht directs the builder to make it a little faster than any previous vessel, and thus the ingenuity of the enterprising builders is taxed to the uttermost, and excellence is the natural result."

This race to magnificence was started not so much by *North Star*, since she was put into commercial service after her grand tour and was not really considered a bona fide yacht by the yachtsmen of the day, as by William H. Aspinwall, president of the Pacific Mail Steamship Co. To test whether a new invention, a single paddle wheel in the interior of a vessel, could be applied to his commercial ships, he had a 60-footer built. The wheel was a flop, but he kept the boat, put side-wheels with feathering buckets on her, named her *Fire-Fly* and began using her as a yacht for commuting from his country place on Staten Island to his Manhattan office. His son John caught the bug, and in a little over thirty years built thirteen steam yachts, working them himself as engineer, pilot and captain. A forerunner of the grander vessels to come was *Sentinel*, a 103-footer. Through these years Jacob Lorillard, who began a policy in 1868 of building a yacht a year and selling her at the end of the season, was also spreading the gospel. His largest was *Tillie*, a 105-footer.

As these gentlemen raced around New York Harbor, up the Hudson and up the Sound at speeds up to a then-astounding 17 knots, they began to attract the attention of men with bigger ideas. E. T. Gerry bought one of Aspinwall's boats, then sold her and built the much fancier 178-foot *Electra* to act as flagship of the New York Yacht Club.

Electra was quite a vessel for her day. The niceties of life were already being considered. Her double smokestack was arranged to carry off the cooking odors from the galley. She had fifty-eight Edison electric lights of 16-candlepower each and 100-candlepower masthead and running lights, a machine that could make 56 pounds of ice a day, ventilation blowers and independent fire and bilge pumps.

In 1881, George Osgood of New York astounded his friends by breakfasting in Newport at 7 A.M. and taking off for New York aboard his 185-foot yacht *Stranger*. At an average speed of 15 knots, he arrived in New York in nine hours, dining there that evening, the 1881 equivalent of lunch in London and dinner in New York in the jet age. She was the fastest yacht that year, but the old urge had started, and soon the same builders, William Cramp and Sons of Philadelphia, had turned out a larger and faster yacht that eclipsed *Stranger*, and her sistership, the first Morgan *Corsair*.

This was Jay Gould's *Atalanta*, a 248-footer capable of more than 20 knots, built in 1883. She also stepped up the luxury of her appointments, which, in her builder's words, were "magnificently fitted up with hardwood saloons and staterooms." Not only that, but she finished 11 minutes ahead of *Stranger* in a 95-mile race from Larchmont to New London when fresh from the yard, and the yachting fraternity had still another standard to meet.

William Astor at least met it in 1884 with the first vessel to use the famous name *Nourmahal* which, incidentally, means "Light of the Harem." Jaffray called this 232-foot Harlan and Hollingsworth production "a queen among steam yachts." A steel vessel, with provisions for sail as a bark, as well as steam, the custom in these early yachts, she was designed for ocean use, and her looks were especially pleasing. Rakish bow, elliptical stern and a long, lean midships section made her shapely as well as sea-kindly, and her glossy, black steel topsides were noted for the smoothness with which the plates were joined. Her female figurehead and the delicate gold tracery at her bow were also admired.

She had one large, black stack, and, as a reminder of what went on in her innards to make the gracious living topsides possible, she had eight coaling ports. Jaffray said she was "of strength sufficient to laugh at the fitful moods of the ocean."

Even these free-wheeling new millionaires had to give some thought to cost, however. Everybody knows what J. P. Morgan, Sr. said when asked about the cost of running a yacht, but it is not so well known that he said it in answer to a question by Henry Clay Pierce, who had

Jay Gould's *Atalanta* set new standards when she was launched

Opposite: *Electra* had many luxury innovations

Electra modernized and in new dress

DECK SALOON.

GRAND SALOON.

ON DECK.

LADIES' SALOON.

OWNER'S STATE ROOM.

PANTRY.

GANGWAY.

THE YACHT NAMOUNA.

OWNER'S DECK ROOM.

SIGNAL GUN.

ENGINE ROOM.

SAFETY VALVE OF ENGINE.

JAMES GORDON BENNETT'S NEW STEAM YACHT NAMOUNA.

[FROM SKETCHES BY OUR SPECIAL ARTIST AND PHOTOGRAPHS BY PACH.]

Namouna was James Gordon Bennett's entry in the luxury sweepstakes

Opposite: Life aboard *Namouna* as pictured in the
New York *Daily Graphic* in April 1882

made his money in oil. Clinton H. Crane, one of the top naval architects of the period, and a man who designed many of the major steam
yachts of the early twentieth century and got to know their owners
well through his dealings with them, gives a postscript to Morgan's
famous answer that "you have no right to own a yacht if you ask
that question."

Pierce, even though he asked about cost, gave no evidence of
worrying about it as he planned his new vessel with Crane. He
wanted special food compartments in the hold, including an elaborate
refrigerating plant, and he also had his quarters done by a Boston
interior decorator all in silk panels with gold-plated hardware, gold
fittings in the bathroom, and altogether some 150 special items.
Smelling trouble, Crane had an order signed by Pierce for every item
specified, which stood him in good stead when the owner finally got
the bills. Forgetting Morgan's dictum, he howled in anguish and

Sir Thomas Lipton in the late 90s

Sir Thomas Lipton's *Erin*

turned the whole batch of bills over to his attorney, but Crane was covered by the signed orders and the bills were paid.

Morgan, Astor, Gould, Gerry and their friends first came out with their big luxury yachts as the nineteenth century was drawing to a close. The salaries they paid their large staffs sound laughable in our inflationary times, but the total bill still came to a tidy sum by the standards of any day. Seamen and firemen received about $30 a month, which was, of course, all found with board and uniforms, and their conditions were much better, in pay and housing, than those of merchant seamen. It was a premium job to work on a yacht. Owners could pick and choose, and most of the crews were Scandinavians with a fine seafaring background. Mates and engineers could get from $45-100 per month, and captains as high as $200. Stewards rated $60-100 and waiters the same as seamen and firemen. The chef could usually command his salary on a personal basis with the owner, who would keep it a secret.

With up to fifty men in the crews of the larger yachts, the monthly payroll could run about $2,500, and it would cost $1,500 to feed them. James Gordon Bennett's *Namouna* was kept in commission year-round, Bennett entertained lavishly, and she was maintained in top condition. She probably cost him about $150,000 a year to run, which is a good solid figure even at Gay Nineties prices. Gould and Astor were said to spend only slightly less, mainly because they didn't entertain as much.

Townsend Perry, writing in the New York *World* of November 8, 1885, summed up an article on the costs of operating a big yacht by saying, "I don't know which will eat a man up the quickest, an extravagant wife or a steam yacht, but think of a rich man with both." The answer to this, however, came from a wealthy yachtsman, who gave this heartfelt endorsement. "My yacht, it is true, has cost a large sum, but it is worth every dollar of it. It has made a new man of me. Before I built it, I was constantly suffering from dyspepsia and other troubles arising from too close attention to business. Now I am a well man."

And so, as a balm to dyspeptic millionaires and an expression of their desire for regal trappings and ego-extensions, yachting had become a colorful facet of the life of the era by the the time the nineteenth century gave way to the twentieth. The America's Cup competition made yacht-racing a glamorous sport, virtually the first international one, and the figures involved in it received as much attention as movie stars, TV stars, and sports champions do today, becoming almost household words. In fact Sir Thomas Lipton did a fantastically astute job of making his name and his tea one, in a public relations performance that was far ahead of its time, and still ranks as one of the most effective from both a sporting and a commercial standpoint.

The luxury yachts that trailed in the wake of the glamorous Cup yachts also became famous in themselves, a part of the American scene, and a true expression of the country's prosperity and growing economic power. The Goulds, Astors, Morgans, Vanderbilts, Gerrys, Bennetts, Lorillards and their fellow members in the club didn't just become famous because they owned big yachts, but their vessels kept them in the public eye, glamorized them and gave them a status that business figures had not known before.

With their luxurious craft, they set a style and established traditions that flourished and increased through those last "days of innocence" that preceded World War I. Luxury yachting reached a peak in these years that it was never to know again on the same scale.

The sport had grown enough for three monthly magazines devoted to yachts to set up shop: *Rudder* in 1890, *Motor Boating* in 1906 and *Yachting* in 1907. While they paid attention to the small launches and sailboats that were coming into use as pleasure craft, the luxury yachts were what filled their pages with a fascination like that of the movie magazines of the 20s and 30s. Few could climb the companionway up the glossy sides of a *Nourmahal* or *Corsair*, but they could glimpse the wonders of her interior in the pages of the magazines.

By 1914 a tradition had been established, one that was to continue to grow for another thirty years, and then change and mushroom in very different fashion. To go into the particulars of how this tradition started and then grew calls for a return to the year 1816.

The German royal yacht *Hohenzollern*

The Empress's bedroom in *Hohenzollern*. Evidently she needed help in staying in her bunk, from the way the chairs are placed.

Hohenzollern's grand saloon—well suited to royal entertaining

Cleopatra's Barge in the harbor of Civitavecchia

2

Cleopatra's Barge

Long before the floating palaces of the nineteenth-century million-aires brought a new definition and dimension to the word "yachting," America had a true luxury yacht. She was called *Cleopatra's Barge*, a vessel frankly dedicated to out-and-out luxury and pleasure, and she came from the unlikely surroundings of the rockbound New England Coast. The port of Salem, just north of Boston, with its heritage of witch-burning and Puritanism, had changed as it developed into a world port. Salem ships brought luxury items, and profits from the Orient, Europe and the Caribbean, and Salem merchants were in a position to profit mightily from privateering in the War of 1812.

A good portion of this money came to a family named Crownin-shield, and one of its scions, a fifty-year-old bachelor named George, decided to use some of these not-so-righteously acquired profits in sheer frivolity. He had a 100-foot brig built, fitted her out in the height of a luxury no merchant ship had ever known, and named her *Cleopatra's Barge* so that there would be no doubt about what she was like and what she was intended for. She was to take him and a group of his friends on a high-style grand tour of the Continent.

Even though she was an isolated instance, far ahead of her time in 1816, and not, from any established record, imitating the yachts that were just becoming popular at Cowes, she did set a style, and her owner set a pace, that was copied, sometimes consciously, often unconsciously, by those who came after bachelor George in the pursuit of pleasure afloat. It wasn't the first time a rich man had indulged his whims in lavish living, but it was the first time, at least in the United States of America, that these whims centered on a yacht.

George Crowninshield would have been recognizable in any era for what he was. Short, a mere 5 feet, 6 inches, he had the familiar traits that go with his stature. He was a loud extrovert, and something of a dandy, indulging in little trademarks like a shaggy beaver hat, a seaman's pigtail, and extravagant clothes. When the War of 1812 ended, and his father died, George and his brothers never had to worry about working again. The family's fast 114-foot brigantine *America*, operating as a privateer during the war, had brought back prizes worth over a million dollars, a fantastic sum in that era, to add to the already solid family fortune.

George had spent many years at desks managing the family fortunes, but he had always dreamed of going back to sea. He had already indulged himself with a sailboat that was not intended for utilitarian purposes. In 1801 he had a little sloop called *Jefferson* in which he knocked about the harbor, but she had been sacrificed to the exigencies of the War of 1812 and had been put to work as a privateer. After the war, he had more grandiose ideas. Bored with the circumscribed life at Salem, with his eyes on the delights and luxuries of gentler climes, he saw no reason for spending his declining years counting privateering profits through the dark New England winters. He decided to make his daydreams come true, and the sailing qualities of the fast privateer, *America*, inspired him to duplicate them in a pleasure vessel. Obviously he had read descriptions of the royal barge, canopied in cloth of gold, in which Cleopatra came to meet Marc Anthony, hence the name, an arrant admission of frivolity, but he was an able, experienced seaman who knew that he wanted a good, sound ship.

He didn't have far to go to have her built. Salem was one of the major ports of the country, with a shipbuilding industry to go with this stature. One of the shipyards had been operating for 145 years

18
Legendary
Yachts

George Crowninshield

on the same site. It was established by John Becket in 1655, and his descendent, with an individualistic name of Retire, was operating it when George decided to build his dream vessel. Salem shipbuilders were skilled enough to turn out a premium vessel, soundly built and luxuriously fitted. The bill was $50,000, a scandalous sum for the times, but this was just the basic vessel, before George began to indulge the whims that would make her live up to her name.

Perhaps no perfumed maidens reclined on ottomans along her rails, but Cleopatra would no doubt have delighted in the velvet cushions, elegant settees, mirrors, glass, porcelain, gilt, gold and bronze ornaments and other lavish touches. The main saloon was adorned by a glittering chandelier, and Crowninshield made sure that the glassware, cutlery, mirrors and furniture were as elaborate as any in the finest salons in Boston.

For operation of the vessel, he ordered a complement of sails to include many extra-light ones for Mediterranean conditions, her ropes were coded in different colors for ease in handling, her belaying pins were highly ornamental in brass, and such items as her windlass and her steering gear were the latest patent devices. As an added whimsical touch, each side was painted differently. On her starboard side there was a horizontal pattern in alternating colors, and the port side had a highly individualistic zigzag scheme. Vessels passing on opposite sides of her would report seeing quite a different ship.

She was launched on November 21, 1816, amid festivities that gave Salemites something to talk about through the long winter and for many more months. There was a huge crowd present, and George was in his element as his friends brought gifts, and everybody celebrated. Soon after the launching, the *Barge* was frozen into her berth, but this didn't halt the festivities. Crowninshield had invited the whole town to come aboard and have a look, and this they did, sometimes by the thousands in one day. George reveled in all the attention and spent the winter making sure that everything was in shape for the grand voyage.

Salem was a sobersided community, and most of those who came to look at *Cleopatra's Barge* came out of mere curiosity. George had his intimates, however, for whom the lavish yacht meant more than a sightseeing visit, and gradually he assembled an "owner's party" for the big cruise. A fifty-year-old bachelor no doubt would develop some friendships that might not sit too well with the conventional members of the community, and his sister-in-law, who took great delight in chronicling developments for the benefit of her husband, Benjamin, George's brother, who was away in Washington as President Madison's Secretary of the Navy, stated drily that George's choice of cruising companions "may appear better abroad than they do at home." Even Salem in 1816 had its not-so-secret swingers.

Before the great venture started, there was a shakedown cruise across Massachusetts Bay to Cape Ann, near Gloucester, and the ship's company had no difficulty in getting into the mood for the high-living that was to come. According to Mrs. Benjamin Crowninshield, some of the party had to be put in their sacks before the cruise was over, but George was as happy as a kid with a new toy.

As soon as the weather was good enough, it was time to leave. George had spent the whole winter in preparation, so there was little more to be done, and *Cleopatra's Barge* cleared the harbor on March 30, 1817, as the whole town buzzed over the makeup of her passenger list, supposedly in disapproval, but no doubt secretly in a green state of envy.

First stop was the Azores, and the *Barge* sailed better than her name, making a good fast passage, with an April 18 arrival. The voyage went on to Gibraltar, Tangier and Majorca, with each port a triumph, as visitors flocked to the strange vessel that had come with no more purpose than the entertainment of her company.

George was a good name-dropper and name user. His brother-in-law had no doubt used his Washington connections to get some impressive letters of introduction, including one from James Monroe, then Secretary of State, to John Quincy Adams, who was Minister to the Court of St. James at London. Despite the fact that this was thousands of miles from the *Barge's* itinerary, it was definitely an eye-opener of an introduction.

Much of George's pleasure came from entertaining the high and mighty in the style to which he was accustomed. A parade of admirals, chief consuls, princes and their ladies visited aboard and

The starboard side decoration of *Cleopatra's Barge*

Port side had a different decorative scheme

dutifully marvelled at *Cleopatra's Barge's* appointments. Even the most sophisticated of them were impressed by the lavish luxury, but it was a hard job to keep the ship from becoming grubby and overly lived-in with the constant press of more lowly visitors that swarmed aboard.

In Barcelona, no less than 8,000 people were clocked over the gangway, and there was constant wear and tear on the furnishings and decor in all ports. George couldn't bear to see her lose any of her luster, and she was forever being repainted, re-fitted and re-decorated during the cruise. The visitors thought nothing of bouncing on the fancy settees, fingering all the precious objects and decorative geegaws, partaking of some wine and asking the price of everything.

The smells and manners of the crowding visitors made life a bit awkward for the ship's company, and George's nephew Ben, son of the Secretary of the Navy, began to be downright anti-social about the whole thing. When some of the visiting ladies became actively seasick as the vessel lurched at anchor, it was almost too much for him, and he grew increasingly disenchanted with the venture. The ship's guests were forever bumping into the wet paint as constant touch-up became George's obsession, and life was further disrupted in Marseilles when a horde of craftsmen came aboard to redecorate much of the interior. New cushions, new tasseled curtains, additional gold leaf and some more practical changes in the ship's gear were all part of the overhaul as Ben became less and less happy with the proceedings. In his journal he began to refer sarcastically to his uncle as "My Lord," and he finally parted company at Gibraltar instead of making the return voyage.

Not that the ship's company wasn't having fun. Each port was a new party, with new V.I.P.s to meet, entertain and be entertained by, and the playful guests enjoyed twitting visitors about some of the curious Americana that was so strange to European eyes. A life-size "Cigar Store Indian" in full war paint that rode on deck was a particular eye-opener to sightseers and various stories were made up to suit each new occasion. Some visitors thought it was alive at first, and others were told it was an American saint and kissed its feet.

All was not partying and nonsense. Some of the guests were truly

Cleopatra's Barge under way

enjoying shipboard life, even when they were away from port and underway at sea, and various journals kept during the voyage reflect the excitement of offshore sailing, of which most of them had had no experience before. The sight of phosphorous in the wake, of porpoises playing around the bow wave, and of stars wheeling overhead at night mixed with the impressions of strange ports and strange people.

George couldn't have been happier. He was in his element, and as far as he was concerned, the minor mishaps that would inevitably dog such an unprecedented venture were mostly good for a laugh. He acquired some paintings that proved not to be the old masters he took them for. Fleas were brought aboard by Italian visitors, and it was hard to keep the food supply from deteriorating.

His grand moment came, however, when he traveled to Rome and was a guest of the Bonapartes. He was ready after that to head back for Massachusetts before the North Atlantic weather became too boisterous, and once his grouchy nephew Ben was put ashore at Gibraltar the return voyage went smoothly enough.

This was the life for George. Poor little Salem paled beside the wonders of the great wide world and the attention that *Cleopatra's Barge* could get him in exotic ports. He came home only to plan another voyage the following season. This would take him to Northern Europe, where Scandinavians would probably be even more amazed than citizens of the Mediterranean world at the sight of a vessel whose only purpose was frivolous luxury. With it all, she had been well-handled as a ship. The Crowninshield tradition, the Salem tradition, for first-rate seafaring had been upheld. She might have been a social anomaly in the dead-serious world of 1817, but she was no nautical freak. If she had been, she would never have made it across the ocean and back.

George's dreams came quickly to an end, however. No doubt the life he had led and the tendency of his short frame to stoutness contributed to a heart attack that killed him a month and a half after the end of the unique voyage. He was on board his beloved *Barge* when he died on November 26, and who knows what further influence the unusual vessel might have had, hastening by many years the start of luxury yachting in the United States, if she had been operated by George in his inimitable, flamboyant manner for a few more years. Jealous imitators would have been sure to follow much sooner than the 1840s, when yachting in America finally began to take hold.

Cleopatra's Barge and *Jefferson* were put up for auction the next summer to settle George's estate, and the *Barge* went for $15,400, as plain a commentary as any on the demand for $50,000 luxury yachts in the year 1818. She was converted to merchant-ship duty, was re-sold in 1820 and seemed doomed to an anonymous end in the merchant trade, but she was saved for one final symbolic moment of glory.

Her 1820 owners sent her on a voyage to the Sandwich Islands, the civilized name for the islands the natives called Hawaii, and her special glamor was not lost on King Kamehameha II. He was at the height of a reign that was grandiose in its own way, before white settlers gradually ate away the power of native royalty in the islands, and he decided that the smart little vessel would make a perfect royal yacht. He negotiated a sale price to be paid in sandalwood, but unfortunately, the Sandwich Islanders were not skilled in handling a ship with the *Barge's* complicated rigging. Great seamen in their own outrigger canoes and catamarans, they weren't up to operating the *Barge*, and soon after the King took possession of her she was wrecked on a reef.

For a while, there was no yachting in America on a scale like this, but a yacht named *America* finally gave the sport the single biggest push it has ever received.

A contemporary painting of *America* sailing to victory

3

America

America pulled off the impossible. She not only lived up to her name, she even added luster to it. There was a great measure of self-confidence in the action of Commodore John Cox Stevens and his syndicate which gave the name *America* to the schooner they commissioned for the purpose of challenging British yachting supremacy. As the representatives of a nation, they dared to take her into the heart of the "Establishment" of a supremely successful and proud maritime nation. The brash, put-up-or-shut-up challenge from the supposedly uncivilized new nation startled the British, and the ship's overwhelming success became even more significant because of the boastful way in which she was named.

The cup she won, which Commodore Stevens brought back and eventually put into international competition as a challenge cup named for her, became the single most important trophy in yachting, and it no doubt would not have had this wide influence if she had been named *Wave* or *Gimcrack* like earlier Stevens vessels. Imagine the whole world hanging on the outcome of the Gimcrack's Cup! That it was called the America's Cup, even if this was only a boat name and not actually the land itself, gave it that extra something that has made it a household word, and the one yachting trophy that is widely known outside the sport.

Much has been written about this single most influential yacht in history. Several books, countless magazine articles, and even a TV special, have told her story. The replica built for the TV program has made her even more familiar by making appearances at many yachting events and in the yachting centers of two hemispheres, but well-known as she is, no book on great yachts would be complete without including her. She holds a unique place in yachting history.

To John Cox Stevens, she was the culmination of many years of experimentation with racing sailboats. Since boyhood, when he had first built model boats to sail on the Hudson River off the Stevens family home at Castle Point, Hoboken, N.J., Stevens had spent much of his time building and racing boats. Son of an early steamboat pioneer in a family of brilliant inventors, his main interest was in sail, and his first boat, a 20-footer named *Diver*, was built in 1809 when he was 24. He experimented with a catamaran, then reverted to single hulls with the schooners *Wave, Onkahye* and *Gimcrack*. The New York Yacht Club, oldest in the United States, was formed in *Gimcrack's* cabin in 1844.

Despite this distinction, Stevens wasn't satisfied with her when she took a third in the club's first regatta, and the family pooled forces to produce a winner. Brother Robert designed a 92-foot sloop, named *Maria* for John's wife, which John and his brother Edward raced, and for years she was the fastest boat in New York Harbor, the sport's first racing machine.

Success with *Maria* brought dreams of wider horizons to the Stevenses, and these horizons opened up with the plans for the 1851 Crystal Palace exposition in England. Many special events, including yacht racing, were scheduled around this first of the great international expositions, and Stevens formed a syndicate of New York Yacht Club members to build a schooner to sail across and enter. An invitation was received from the Earl of Wilton, Commodore of the Royal Yacht Squadron, for the new yacht to visit the club, but he carefully avoided committing any specific Royal Yacht Squadron yachts to direct competition.

George L. Schuyler, one of the founders of New York Yacht Club, was the syndicate's negotiator in arranging for the design and building of *America*. She was designed by George Steers, who had designed previous yachts for Stevens, and built at the commercial yard of William H. Brown on the Manhattan side of the East River. Steers worked in the classic manner, carving the lines on a wooden model, rather than working on paper.

The lines were taken off full size and laid down on the floor of the mould loft, where Steers then made adjustments by eye, reshaping the long flexible battens used to indicate the lines by kicking them or shimming them, then nailing them down.

In the manner of boat yards since time immemorial, there were delays in building the husky hull, planked with three-inch white oak sides and 2½-inch yellow pine decks over frames of white oak, locust, cedar, chestnut and hackmatack, all copper fastened. Her syndicate wanted her by April 1, but she was built out in the open, with no cover for the workmen, and weather delayed the project. She wasn't launched until May 3, with no special ceremony to celebrate the occasion, and her first sailing trial wasn't until May 17. *Maria* was used as a yardstick, and she beat the new schooner, but not by much. Since she was considered an inshore racing machine, and *America* had to cross the ocean by herself, the results were generally encouraging, and builder Brown finally got $30,000 in mid-June, when she was turned over to the syndicate and almost immediately, on June 21, set off for Europe. The price was $10,000 below the original contract because of late delivery.

She was an unusual vessel in many ways, the first ever to cross an ocean for international competition. She was modeled on the swift schooners that had made a name for themselves off the American coast as they raced out to be the first to greet incoming ships, thereby getting the piloting job. In England, the conventional shape for sailing hulls was known as "cod's head and mackerel tail," a form with bluff, bulbous bows and long, tapering after section, but *America* was just the opposite. Her bow was long and lean, and her greatest beam was just aft of amidships. This gave her a flatter run aft, and she was also stiff and powerful, able to carry a tall rig by the standards of the day. She moved through the water with remarkably little fuss alongside, and a flat, untroubled wake that amazed

America as a Naval Academy practice ship in Boston, 1862

many observers. Because she made so little disturbance passing through the water, even experienced sailors found it hard to believe she was going as fast as she was until they compared her performance with other boats. She had a long, graceful sheer, and distinctively raked masts almost bare of rigging.

For her unprecedented Transatlantic passage she was outfitted with a smaller suit of sails than the ones intended for racing. Her captain was Richard Brown (no relation to the builder), a Sandy Hook pilot with a wealth of schooner experience. He was part-owner of the Sandy Hook pilot boat *Mary Taylor* after which *America* was modeled, and brought a suit of her sails as a cut-down rig for *America's* passage. Steers was aboard but the syndicate members making the trip to England preferred a steamer passage and would join her in France when she outfitted for racing there. Commodore Stevens, his brother Edward, and Colonel James Hamilton, Schuyler's father-in-law, were the afterguard representatives.

The passage to Le Havre took 20 days, 6 hours, a fairly good one considering that there were five days of calm and some light going on other days. Steers' brother James was aboard with his son, who suffered from seasickness and homesickness, coloring his father's diary account of the trip to some extent. James worried most about the food, and his accounts of the menus were more detailed than the sailing reports. The Fourth of July was celebrated by a cessation of all ship's work except for the actual sailing watches, and many toasts were made over a bottle of gin that James Steers gave the crew.

On July 10, *America* logged 250 miles and Steers reported that "the scene is exciting" as the underrigged schooner picked up and passed three full-rigged ships carrying everything they could set. The English Channel pilot who came aboard off the Scilly Isles asked to heave the log himself, as he wouldn't believe that she was doing 12 knots with such a smooth wake.

At Le Havre, she was drydocked for cleaning and painting, and the Stevens brothers and Colonel Hamilton arrived on the scene to take charge. The utilitarian gray paint she had worn for the ocean passage was covered by a glossy black coat, decorated with gold trailboards, and sheer stripe, and a new coat of gold for the eagle on her stern.

Her boom, gaffs and topmasts (she had a loose-footed foresail) were painted white, and her racing sails were bent on. By July 31 she was all shining and sparkling and ready to impress the Royal Yacht Squadron, and she set out across the Channel for Cowes.

Word of her sailing was brought over ahead of her by a Channel steamer, and she was eagerly awaited at the English port. Fog, light wind and a foul tide caused her to anchor for the night about six miles from Cowes, but the next morning everyone at Cowes was up early in hopes of seeing the Yankee clipper arrive. It was on this morning that the tensest moment of her whole visit occurred, and perhaps the most significant of the trip.

While the crowds on shore awaited anxiously, the crew of the crack new British racing cutter *Laverock* couldn't wait, and they made their way to *America's* anchorage, circling her as soon as she began to make sail in a light westerly and the first of a favorable tide. Commodore Stevens didn't really want to test his yacht under these circumstances, as she was heavily loaded with stores, "enough for an East India voyage" as he put it in telling of the incident at a yacht club dinner back home the next fall. It was too much of a challenge to resist, however. There was *Laverock* sniffing around like a chesty dog in its own yard, obviously spoiling for a brush, and it would have been almost impossible to avoid the encounter. As it turned out, this was something of a mistake, but the satisfactions were still many, both short term and long range.

Silently, with no acknowledgment that any contest was involved, but with everyone for miles around knowing it, *America's* crew got her sails up and weighed anchor, with *Laverock* about 200 yards ahead. For a breathless five minutes no one moved on deck as Captain Brown crouched down at the tiller and coaxed the black schooner into the groove. The only sound was the slight whisper of water past her sharp stem as every man on board glued his eyes on *Laverock's* stern. Were they gaining or dropping back?

It didn't take long to find out. It was soon obvious that *America* had more speed. She worked across *Laverock's* wake and up to windward, and by the time the vessels reached Cowes, she was between a quarter and a half mile ahead. All eyes were on her as she rounded

A British picturization of *America* after her victory

up to anchor off the Royal Yacht Squadron clubhouse, and soon the Earl of Wilton, the Marquis of Anglesey and other prominent yachtsmen came aboard. They were there to extend greetings, but they also looked the strange new vessel over with very curious eyes.

Some excuses were made for *Laverock*—supposedly she had been slowed by towing her tender—but the word spread quickly that the American vessel was not to be taken lightly, and the great sportsmen of British yachting were very slow to present any challenge to her. In fact, challenges or opportunities for competition were non-existent. Much of the competition of the day was arranged by wagers between owners, but Commodore Stevens couldn't find any local money willing to go against the glossy black schooner. When there was a formal regatta, some excuse was made about the visitor's eligibility, though she went out unofficially and sailed away from the fleet on one occasion.

Finally, not for money, which Stevens really wanted, to recoup the expenses of the venture, but for an ornate bottomless ewer known as the Royal Yacht Squadron 100 Guineas Cup, she was allowed to enter an open regatta that the Royal Yacht Squadron was running on August 22. This was to be a complete circuit of the Isle of Wight, a 53-mile course through difficult waters, a poor place for a fair race. Tide piloting and many tricks of local knowledge are vital for negotiating the route around the squashed diamond of an island, and there was also a suspicion of some team racing when the contest actually started. Her entry was assured when *The Times* of London wrote a scathing article about lack of British sportsmanship, shaming the Royal Yacht Squadron into allowing her to enter.

It had been a difficult time for *America's* crew. The tensions over the idleness and lack of competition, and the social pressures of keeping up with titled Englishmen, and even royalty, had caused a rift between the Steers brothers, who felt they were being slighted and pushed aside socially, and the bluff Commodore and his afterguard. The expedition was about to dissolve into petty squabbling and major disappointments until the chance to prove the vessel finally came.

No doubt Commodore Stevens was disappointed that he had been unable to take any money from the cautious Squadron members, but the fact that he won that bottomless ewer and put it back into competition has given him a place in history that no amount of winnings from wagering could have done.

The race gave *America* a chance to prove everything that had been hoped for her by the Americans and feared about her by the British. *The Times* reported that "a large portion of the peerage and gentry of the United Kingdom left their residences and forsook the sports of the moors to witness the struggle. . . . All the feelings of that vast population which swarms in our southern ports and firmly believes in Rule Britannia as an article of national faith; all the prejudices of the wealthy aristocracy and gentry who regarded the beautiful vessels in which they cruised about the Channel and visited the shores of the Mediterranean every summer, as the perfection of naval architecture, were roused to the highest degrees, and even the Queen of England did not deem the occasion unworthy of her presence."

There was more about pride in England's yacht building and the pre-eminence of her designers and sailors, and of her clubs, and the article went on to say, "till the *America* came over, the few who were aware that there was a flourishing club in New York did not regard it as of the slightest consequence, or as likely to interfere with their monopoly of the glory of the manliest and most useful of all sports."

Cowes was jammed with yachts and people in a festive mood, and this was, at that moment, the most significant event in the history of the sport. Shamed by *The Times* and caught up in the spirit of big-time doings, a record entry of eighteen had signed up for the race. It was to be an open event, with no handicaps, and the start was from anchor, moored in a double row off Cowes Castle. Only fifteen actually started when the gun sounded at ten o'clock on a warm, hazy forenoon. The sun had burned off the mists of early morning, and a light westerly wind was filling in as the fleet scrambled to get underway.

America was last off. As though deigning unseemly haste and biding their time, her crew were slow in making sail and weighing anchor, but finally the flat, well-cut American sails of cotton, a contrast to the baggy flax sails of the British boats, filled and took shape. She had been overriding her anchor in the tideway when trying to

America returned to yacht racing after the War Between the States

weigh it under sail, so all sail had to be lowered before the anchor would come up. In a quarter of an hour, she had already managed to pass all but three of the boats, and, on the first puffs of a freshening breeze, she passed all but *Gipsey Queen*, which had started under a great press of sail.

The boats then fell into a flat spot and *America's* sails went limp. The little *Volante* was charging up from astern with what *The Times's* man called a "stupendous jib swallowing up all the wind that was blowing," and she picked a dramatic moment to sweep by into the lead, as the fleet was just then passing Osborne House, the Queen's summer residence. The yachts made a brave sight spread, with their retinue of spectator craft, from shore to shore against a backdrop of the green hills of Hampshire. *Volante* held her lead passing the jammed pier at Ryde and on to No Man's Land buoy, where they began to meet the swells from the open Channel. The breeze was freshening and they were bowling along beautifully. With *Volante*, *Freak*, *Aurora* and *Gipsey Queen* all still ahead of *America*, with two minutes separating *Volante* and the schooner, British hearts beat a bit faster, and some of the less nautically knowledgeable spectators thought that *America's* feared threat might not be so fierce after all.

Not the sailors watching, however, as they took note of what happened as the breeze freshened. Standing straight and surging ahead powerfully as each puff hit her, she picked off boat after boat and finally caught *Volante* at 1130, just as they were ready to round onto the wind for a close-hauled fetch along the back of the island. This was where the superior cut of her flatter sails began to show, and the action of her hull in a sea also became very apparent. While the bluff-bowed Britishers were throwing spray from forward as they thrashed through the chop, *America* sliced gracefully along, completely dry on deck, with a clean flash of water along her shining topsides. The press steamer had trouble keeping up with her here, and she soon had the fleet tucked away to leeward, almost hull down.

This was actually the best sailing of the whole race. As they rounded the bottom of Wight's "diamond" the wind fell light and *America's* crew, with a little over-enthusiastic trimming with the windlass, broke her jibboom. It was a long beat to the westward from

General Butler kept *America* as a family yacht for many years

here. With *America* gaining steadily despite the mishap, competition gradually fell away. Some boats just quit, *Arrow* managed to run aground while rock-hopping out of the tide along the shore, and *Freak* fouled *Volante* in some bow-to-bow action as these two and *Aurora* also tried the inshore route, tacking at close quarters. *Volante*, considered the best light air threat to *America*, carried away her jib-boom in the collision and was out of it.

For a while the breeze freshened again, then fell very light in late afternoon. The spectator steamers went on ahead to Alum Bay, near The Needles at the entrance to the Solent, to await the yachts, and, coming the other way down the Solent from Osborne, there was the stately royal yacht *Victoria and Albert* with the Queen, Prince Consort and Prince of Wales visible on deck. The royal yacht anchored near the spectator steamers, giving them an extra thrill on this day of special thrills, and a small boat soon took the Prince Consort and his son (eventually Edward VII), suitably dressed in a sailor suit, in to the beach for a walk up the cliffs. With the young prince gamboling about, they started up the path, where many spectators had gathered, only to have a sudden patch of wet drizzle blowing in from sea drive them back to the yacht's shelter.

America finally drifted past at 1830 and *Victoria and Albert* followed along close aboard. Though it was considered as unusual for a yacht to render a salute while racing as for a jockey to tip his hat to the Queen while flashing by the royal box at Ascot, *America* with the competition hull down astern, lowered her ensign, the Commodore doffed his hat, and the crew stood with uncovered heads. *The Times* called this a "mark of respect for the Queen not the less becoming because it was bestowed by republicans."

Although there is no record of it, this is probably the occasion for the legendary exchange when the Queen asked who was leading and who was second and was supposedly told, "Your Majesty, there is no second." There was actually a quote like this in *The Times's* story, but it was attributed to the general hails being passed about at Cowes when those who had been following the race came back there. *America*, sliding through the summer twilight on the lightest of zephyrs, made it to the finish at 2037 to the salute of gunfire. *Aurora*, smallest boat in the race, had benefited from the drifting conditions, and also picked up a new evening breeze at The Needles, and came on fast to close the gap to finish at 2055, and only three more boats even had their time taken.

There was no handicapping for the race, but had the system then in use been applied, *America* would have saved her time on *Aurora* by two minutes.

And so she had achieved her moment of supreme glory, and the rest of her story is all really aftermath, but there are some interesting sidelights to it.

First of all, the cup might never have come over here at all if a protest had been upheld. Mr. Ackers, owner of *Brilliant*, the largest entry, and the last one to be timed (at 0120 August 23), entered a protest against the cup being awarded to *America* on the grounds that she had not rounded The Nab when leaving Spithead, which was usually a mark of the round-the-island race. However, it had not been specified as a mark in this race, and most of the fleet followed *America* along an inshore route that could have been dangerous at certain stages of the tide. What an impact on yachting history, or rather lack of it, there would have been if there had been a "homer" decision on this protest! No cup, no America's Cup competition, and all those millions of dollars would not have been spent and all those reputations would not have been made. Fortunately, the gentlemen of the Royal Yacht Squadron *were* gentlemen and disallowed the protest on the rightful grounds that rounding The Nab had not been in the instructions. On such small decisions history sometimes turns.

The Queen and Prince Consort were interested enough to pay a visit to *America* at Cowes, where she rode at anchor in triumph, surrounded by hundreds of the curious in small boats, launches and almost anything that floated. The Queen was very impressed with the vessel's cleanliness and had a lesson in how it was achieved, when Captain Brown politely asked the Prince to wipe the mud off his boots before being shown below. The Queen tested the cleanliness of the galley by wiping her lace handkerchief over the counter. She gave the crew gold sovereigns and sent Captain Brown a gold pocket compass as a memento.

The replica of *America* passes The Needles while re-creating the sail around the Isle of Wight in 1968

British yachtsmen also swarmed aboard to study the phenomenon's secrets, and, a few days later, when she had to be hauled, there was a big throng in attendance. Many were there in hopes of seeing some secret underwater propulsion device that had been rumored as the means of making her so fast, while serious connoisseurs of naval architecture studied her lines with much interest.

Commodore Stevens finally got his wish for a wager by arranging a match race with the schooner *Titania*, which *America* won easily, and this £100 bet and the bottomless ewer are the only concrete items she won that summer. The syndicate sold her to an Englishman for $25,000, so that the expedition was not a loss, since expenses had come to just under $4,000.

Renamed *Camilla*, she had various British owners, ended up back in the Civil War as the Confederate vessel *Memphis*, was scuttled and retaken by the North, renamed *America* and used as a blockade vessel. After the war she was a training ship for Annapolis midshipmen, and a crew from the Naval Academy sailed her in the big fleet that turned out for the first defense of the cup against *Cambria* in 1870. This was supposed to duplicate the conditions of *America's* feat of sailing against a fleet in foreign waters. She was fourth, a creditable showing for a nineteen-year-old vessel.

After that, she spent nineteen years as a private yacht in the family of General Edward Butler and was an East Coast fixture. After his death, a group of yachtsmen bought her near-derelict hulk and gave it to Annapolis as a gift to the nation. She was on exhibit there until the exigencies of World War II forced neglect on her. There was no room for a rotting sailing hull in emergency wartime budgets, and she deteriorated rapidly, finally having to be broken up when a snow-heavy shed collapsed on her and almost did the job in one swoop.

In 1967, Rudolph Schaefer of Larchmont, N.Y., an active yachtsman who had, among his many triumphs, a Bermuda Race win in 1936 to his credit, worked out a plan to build a replica of *America* to star in the documentary program his brewing company was to sponsor on television. Her lines were translated for modern builders by Olin Stephens, who had designed many of the defenders of her cup, and she was built lovingly and with fine, traditional craftsmanship by the Goudy and Stevens yard in East Boothbay, Me. (The recurrence of many Stevenses and Stephenses in her story seems an odd coincidence.) She was launched on May 3, 1967, the 116th anniversary of the original launching, with much more pomp and circumstance this time, while bunting streamed in the bright slanting sunshine. A fresh, cool northwester chased clouds away just before evening high tide made it possible to slide her into the Damariscotta River. As a band blared and tootled, sirens sounded and the horns and whistles of a big fleet of yachts and workboats filled the crisp air, she rushed swiftly into her element and floated amid the smaller craft swarming around.

In the jaunty rake of her masts, the proud sweep of her sheer, and the bright glint of sunlight shining off her glossy black sides, one could easily imagine how her predecessor must have looked as the cynosure of all eyes at Cowes when she rode there proudly basking in the glory of a triumph that, even as sweet as it was at the time, and as exciting as it seemed, went far beyond the most grandiose expectations any of her owners or crew could have had.

Alva of the 1890s

4

The Vanderbilts

The three most famous names in the era of the great yachts were Astor, Vanderbilt and Morgan. Because they spanned more generations in their prominence and carried family traditions in the grand manner on longer, they are the best remembered and have left the strongest mark. The Astors and Morgans added to the sense of continuity by carrying on a single name for successive big yachts through the generations. The Vanderbilts, though they were a generation behind the Astors socially, were the first to start yachting, with the European junket of the Commodore's *North Star* in 1853. They also had more family members active in yachting and a variety of yacht names. They used *North Star* several times and also made *Alva*, *Winchester*, *Ara*, *Vagrant* and several others into standards. In addition, the personal feats of Harold S. Vanderbilt, the most successful skipper in America's Cup history, continued to keep the family name prominently in the fore of yachting.

The Vanderbilt story is therefore a diversified one, and the family feuds, multi-marriages and front page doings in other spheres have added complications to their yachting activities. There was a nautical tradition in the family long before yachting days. Their eventual dominance in the transportation field—in ferries, steamships and railroads—began in a ferry service that Cornelius Vanderbilt, the original of the many "Commodores" in the family, ran from Staten Island to Manhattan in the early nineteenth century. A farm boy from the island, he started his service at the age of sixteen in 1810, carrying farm produce and passengers, and he expanded it during the War of 1812 by supplying military installations around the harbor.

In 1817 he switched to steam and for twelve years was captain of a ferry to New Brunswick, N.J. Gradually he acquired other ferries and coastwise vessels until his fleet was large enough for him to be called "Commodore," even though it was just a courtesy title that pleased him, not an official rank. Later generations of "Commodore Vanderbilts" picked up the title formally via the New York Yacht Club and other clubs.

In 1849, the Commodore received a charter from Nicaragua to operate a stage route across its isthmus, carrying gold seekers on their way to California, and by 1853 he was worth $11,000,000, the largest private fortune in America at the time, since John Jacob Astor's death in 1848 had spread his fortune to heirs. To dramatize it to those who felt that the rough-and-ready Commodore was not yet eligible for New York society, he built a 270-foot paddle steamboat, mammoth for the time, the first real steam yacht in the U.S., and, expanding on the Crowninshield tradition of thirty-five years previous, he set out on a grand tour of Europe in the lavish vessel.

The tyrannical, hard-nosed Commodore had made no friends in his ruthless rise to fortune, but he had a big family, and it filled *North Star's* ten luxurious staterooms, whose berths were veiled in lace curtains. His wife and ten of his twelve children, seven sons-in-law, one friend of a daughter and a ship's physician and chaplain, each with wives, filled out the passenger list. Some of the deck crew were sons of prominent families along for the lark, but the stokers were professionals, and when the black room gang struck for higher wages an hour before scheduled departure, May 19, they were quickly dismissed, and the captain was told to round up what hands he could to take their place.

Despite a couple of groundings, and despite the Commodore's overbearing manner and seaman's ability to curse, the cruise was a resounding success, attracted wide attention, and set a tradition that rich Americans, and particularly the Vanderbilt family, were to follow ever after. She covered over 15,000 miles in four months of cruising (she could steam at almost 15 knots with her big 34-foot-diameter paddles), visiting Scandinavia, the British Isles, France, Spain and the Mediterranean.

North Star didn't remain a yacht long. She was converted to pasenger service on her return, and the Commodore returned to adding to his fortune with considerable success. Shifting from steamships to railroads in the mid-50s, he had built it to $40,000,000 by his death in 1877. His son William Henry, no yachtsman, but always in awe of his crusty parent, also inherited his love for fortune-building and more than doubled it in the few years before he died in 1885. This provided an excellent base for the next generation to move into the yachting big time in expansive fashion. The two main branches of William Henry's family, caught in a family feud of varied ramifications, went their separate ways in yachting.

William Henry's son Cornelius was not a yachtsman, but another son, William Kissam, was. His yacht was the *Alva*, in which he matched the Astors, Morgans, Goulds, Bennetts et al., and did a great deal of cruising in the late nineteenth century and the early twentieth, but Cornelius, who died in 1899, had a son also named Cornelius, who spent much of his life in yachts. It was this Cornelius Vanderbilt, who lived from 1875 to 1942, whose wife became the imposing *Grande Dame* of New York society, and whose "cottage," Beaulieu, was one of Newport's showplaces. It was also this Cornelius who became involved in a celebrated feud with his father over his marriage, and they never spoke thereafter. Mrs. Vanderbilt was a Wilson, a proud millionairess in her own right, and it is ironic in the extreme that theirs was one of the few Vanderbilt marriages that never broke up. Most of the others married early and often, but, despite all sorts of difficulties and a virtually complete estrangement at the end, when Cornelius retired to his yacht *Winchester* and almost never saw the rest of his family, this marriage was not dissolved. For a while Cornelius had a *North Star*, named for his grandfather's yacht, and he also owned the schooner *Atlantic*, but his last

North Star carried on the original name in the early twentieth century

A stateroom on *North Star*

North Star's dining saloon

All the comforts of home on *North Star*

days were spent on the long, lean, destroyer-like *Winchester*, an extremely fast craft that looked more like a naval vessel than a yacht.

It was this branch of the family that, in addition to the feud between Cornelius and his father, developed the celebrated custody case over Gloria Vanderbilt, daughter of Cornelius's brother Reggie, and one needed a scorecard, a *Social Register* and the latest copies of the gossip columns in the New York press to know which of this tribe of Vanderbilts, Whitneys, Paysons, Furnesses and assorted short liasons-by-marriage were speaking to each other.

A fourth Cornelius, son of this stormy marriage, has told in his memoirs of the difficulties of trying to stay in communication. His mother liked to be in Newport, but his father preferred to stay on his yachts most of the time and often cruised to Europe in them. He disapproved of his son's career as a newspaper man and foreign correspondent, and also of the fact that young Cornelius was an ardent admirer of "That Man" Franklin Delano Roosevelt and worked for him on unofficial assignments.

When the old man's heart began to give him trouble in the late 30s, his wife decided that he should have an elevator in Beaulieu instead of climbing the stairs. One summer day he arrived at Newport in *Winchester* and came ashore in his usual costume of dark blue double-breasted suit, straw "boater" hat with the royal blue, red and white New York Yacht Club colors on the band, the red and white in a thin center stripe, and carrying a rubber-tipped walking stick. When he arrived at the elevator, with his wife and son anxiously anticipating his reaction, he came to a dramatic halt, raised his stick and pointed at the new machine, bellowing, "I suppose you put this in the house hoping it would fall and I would be killed in it, you and your son." With that, he stalked from the house, back to his yacht, never to return to Beaulieu, leaving his son to console the sobbing *Grande Dame* of society.

From then on he remained almost exclusively aboard *Winchester* as his health and mental ability failed. He was under the care of a doctor, and a six-member committee of other family members passed on who would be allowed aboard to see him. His son found it almost impossible to see his father thereafter. Even after rowing

Cornelius Vanderbilt   William Kissam Vanderbilt

out to *Winchester* in a heavy rainstorm in a Long Island harbor, he was refused permission to board.

Winchester was taken to Miami, where Vanderbilt spent his last years, finally moving to a houseboat moored near the yacht of tinplate heir William B. Leeds. Occasionally the two of them walked together through Bayfront Park. Vanderbilt finally succumbed in 1942, the last of his side's line of descent in the family to have a luxury yacht in commission. With World War II already on, it was well beyond the end of an era.

Let us return to William Henry, the non-yachting heir of the original Commodore. The other side of the line of descent in his family was even more prominent in yachting than the Cornelius line. The first William Kissam brought the family back to the big time with *Alva* and took up again the family tradition of cruises to Europe and the entertainment of royalty and society on his vessel. Like his cousin's son Cornelius, he used his yacht for business meetings as well as for social entertaining, as a yacht was the best way for a group of prominent financiers to get off by themselves and work out their dealings without interruption. Cornelius Vanderbilt had many dealings with Charles S. Schwab, who could not be invited to the New York Yacht Club, where business confabs were often held, because he was Jewish, but there was no objection to inviting him to a conference on *Winchester*. That long-standing policy of the New York Yacht Club became defunct in the 1960s, incidentally.

Alva, which means "dawn of day" and was named for Mrs. Vanderbilt, was launched in Wilmington, Del., in 1886, and at 285 feet and a price of $500,000 was the largest and costliest yacht ever built in the country at that time. Her clipper-bowed hull was of mild steel, and she was rigged as a three-masted topsail schooner. Her dining saloon was in white enamel and gold, and each of her staterooms had its own type of hardwood furniture. The 16- by 18-foot library was in French walnut. A private train brought the Vanderbilt party from New York for the gala launching, which was witnessed by a crowd of over 10,000 lining the banks of the creek at the boatyard.

The British Royal Family influence evident
in Cornelius Vanderbilt's dress and pose

It was estimated that operating her took $5,000 a month, and she was soon off on a round of entertaining and cruising, after a shakedown voyage to New York. One of the first gatherings aboard was a meeting of a group known as the Whist Club, of which J. P. Morgan was a member. Her first cruise out of the country was to the West Indies and then she was taken to Europe. In 1888 she went through the Mediterranean as far as Constantinople, where she was a sensation in an area that had seldom seen yachts of this magnitude.

William Kissam's two sons, William K., Jr. and Harold Stirling, both became deeply imbued with yachting traditions in their boyhood voyaging on *Alva* and went on to make quite a name for themselves in the sport in very different ways. William K., Jr., invariably known as Willie, was a serious seaman and cruising yachtsman who spent much of his life cruising to distant ports, and in the process he engaged in a significant amount of oceanographic studies, as well as in dredging for ancient artifacts. His yachts were first class seagoing vessels and were equipped with special instruments for oceanographic work.

Also, like almost any wealthy young man of the era, he couldn't avoid racing, both in sail and power. He was equally interested in fast cars, and often frightened his sailing friends by the way he maneuvered around any horse and wagon traffic in his way. To naval architect Clinton Crane he explained that he could always look between the horse's legs to see if anything was coming, but Crane remained thoroughly scared every time Willie drove him.

An early vessel of Willie's was *Tarantula*, a fast steam yacht on torpedo boat lines. She wasn't the fastest thing afloat, though, and Willie came to Crane to have new boilers designed. They were a success in adding to her speed, but they also caused her to throw a terrific wake at top speed. In passaging the East River, she became the target of numerous claims for damage done by her wake to boats loading at the piers, and to shore property, and she soon developed such a reputation that every claim for wake damage was almost automatically placed against her. Vanderbilt's lawyers were kept continually busy just proving that she hadn't been in the East River at the time of such-and-such a claim.

Ara

Harold S. Vanderbilt's *Vara*, August 1937

Crane called him a shy young man with a very agreeable personality. They raced together on a Herreshoff 70-footer named *Virginia* when Vanderbilt was Commodore of Seawanhaka Corinthian Yacht Club in 1904. Vanderbilt proved an alert, eager sailor, preventing a serious accident by catching the mainsheet just in time when one of the crew freed it in error. His real love was cruising, however, and he was soon at it in earnest. In 1908 he was loaned his father's boat for a long cruise in Greece, and after the World War I hiatus he went at it on a grand scale with his own big yacht, *Ara. Ara* wasn't the conventional glossy luxury yacht. Though she was fitted out in the most comfortable manner, Vanderbilt selected her for her construction and seagoing qualities. She had been built by Camper & Nicholson in England in 1917 as a "sloop-of-war" for blockade service and was 213 feet long, with Polar diesels that gave her 14½ knots and a range of 6,000 miles. Her hull was of ½-inch steel plating.

On January 30, 1921, she set out from New York on a typical Vanderbilt grand-style cruise to Europe. Most of Willie Vanderbilt's cruises were recorded in privately published books that excerpted the log, with additional side comments by the owner and guests. Vanderbilt was her in-fact captain, fully qualified to run the ship and do the navigation, and the Transatlantic passage was shrugged off in the cruise record with a comment on how he had "crossed so many times." She had sails to steady her and the winter passage to the Mediterranean was not an uncomfortable trip. The guests boarded at Villefranche in the south of France and Mrs. W. S. Hoyt took over the commentary by saying that the compartments on the *Train Bleu* were abominably heated but that the sea was clear and blue when they arrived, and the boat was gay with flowers.

The itinerary was classic—Monaco, Genoa, Leghorn, Civitavecchia, Rome, Naples, Pompeii, Sicily, Dalmatia, Venice, Greece, Constantinople, Rhodes, Sardinia, Corsica, Marseilles, where the guests disembarked, then back to the United States. The main concerns were flies and heat. When they were absent, the stop was considered a success. When they were present, everyone was unhappy. *Ara* had an elelctric horse on deck for exercise, there were musicals and card games, and Willie also showed movies of past cruises, such as a jaunt to the Galapagos.

They were momentarily taken aback by being stopped by armed guards in Sardinia, but it was clean and flyless and all was therefore forgiven. Vesuvius at night, with its crater aglow, and the dramatic island of Stromboli and its volcano were memorable sights, and there were always amusing little incidents to liven up the cruise. In Brindisi the ship's company spent an energetic shore visit teaching a bartender to make sidecar cocktails, and in Venice, when they hired a band to come alongside in the evening for atmospheric music, they got three. The cacophony and the argument over the bill made them wary the next time, and when they got to Greece they were careful to shoo serenaders away. It was so hot in Greece—112 at Piraeus, the hottest since 1868—that everyone slept on deck, and the flies were a bother too. A schooner they saw here was the first yacht they had seen since the Riviera.

There was a little excitement when *Ara* was hit by some Greek naval target practice (without damage) but the fact that it was the Fourth of July made it seem more appropriate. After the conditions in some of the ports they had visited, all were delighted to get to the Grand Bretagne Hotel in Athens for a meal, and Willie termed it "the best service since the Automat."

Ara had several three-pounders mounted on deck for her protection in uncertain waters and the Turks at Constantinople at first took her as an unfriendly invader when she arrived, but they were finally convinced to let her stay, after a great web of red tape had been unraveled. Willie was distressed to find the Sultan's Palace turned into a dance hall since his last visit and to see Turks doing the Charleston and singing "Yes sir, that's my baby" there.

On the homeward passage, one of the ship's quartermasters was shot in a Marseilles tavern (not an unusual occurrence for seafarers in that part of the world), a drunken pilot in Cadiz almost wrecked them, and there was a final bit of excitement when *Ara* put into the French island of St. Pierre, in the Gulf of St. Lawrence, on getting back to North America. In Prohibition, this was a hotbed of smuggling activities, and *Ara*, with her military antecedents and three-

The last *Alva*

pounders, had the look of a revenue cutter to the suspicious islanders. There was a flurry of small boats leaving the harbor and of scurrying about on shore until her identity was established.

For Willie, forty-three that year, the cruise must have been a special success, as he and one of the passengers, Mrs. Rosamond Lancaster Warburton, were married at his mother's chateau in France on September 5 while *Ara* was still in the Mediterranean.

Willie continued to cruise in this fashion to many parts of the world, and also carried on more scientifically-oriented oceanographic work in the West Indies and Pacific. He probably logged as many miles cruising as any private yachtsman ever has.

His younger brother Harold, born in 1884, was more interested in racing than in cruising. The family had often been involved in syndicates for America's Cup yachts and other big racing vessels, and Harold himself "started at the top," always racing in big boats without any indoctrination in small-boat sailing in centerboarders or light day sailers. The keen analytical mind that made him one of the world's great bridge players was well-adapted to the organization and racing of complex racing machines.

With a background in the M Class and other boats in the 80- to 100-foot range, Mike Vanderbilt, as he was known to all who sailed with him, was a natural for the America's Cup competition when this historic series was revived in 1930, using boats built to Class J specifications under the International Rating Rule. For the first time, there would be no time handicaps in the match races for the old mug brought home by *America* in 1851, and the direct, boat-for-boat combat would be much more interesting. It was also ideally suited to Mike Vanderbilt's cool-headed, analytical approach, and he became the dominant figure of the J-boat era.

First with *Enterprise,* as one of her syndicate and her skipper, in 1930, then with *Rainbow* in the same capacities in 1934, and finally as *Ranger's* sole owner and skipper in 1937, he became the only triple winner in the series. *Enterprise* was a superior boat to Sir Thomas Lipton's last *Shamrock,* the fifth, but *Rainbow* was clearly a slower boat than T.O.M. Sopwith's *Endeavour.* Vanderbilt's calm handling of an outclassed boat, with an important assist from sailing

Winchester in various color schemes always resembled a destroyer

Winchester in profile

wizard Sherman Hoyt, whom he depended on to get best boat speed out of the mammoth sloop, especially when under genoa jib, saved what looked like a lost cause in defense of the Cup. His exploits with *Ranger* are related in a later chapter, but aside from these three victories, Vanderbilt made other lasting contributions to the sport of sailing.

He developed a timed starting method that is still used by many experienced skippers, following a pattern away from the line and back to it calculated to put him on the line and moving at best speed when the gun goes off, and he also worked up and campaigned hard for a new code of racing rules. Always a keen student of the rules, and not loath to use them in tight situations, he finally saw his ideas adopted in the 1940s.

Still an active yachtsman into the 1960s, after all others of his clan had given up major participation in the sport, Mike Vanderbilt had several handsome power yachts and motorsailers that were in keeping with the luxury yacht standards of the times, though a far cry from the vessels of his ancestors. The last of what could be classed as the great Vanderbilt yachts, however, was the remarkable 12-Meter Class racing sloop, *Vim.* Even a Vanderbilt couldn't keep up a J-boat like *Ranger* season after season, and in any event there was no one else to race against in this class, so the year after *Ranger's* victory, racing a borrowed 12-Meter on Long Island Sound, he decided to enter this class. He commissioned Olin Stephens, who had worked on *Ranger's* design, to turn out a 12-Meter, and she proved to be much faster than the other Twelves in commission. Vanderbilt took her to England in the summer of 1939, the last year of competition before World War II, and turned in a remarkable string of decisive victories.

After a long period of war-enforced inactivity, *Vim* came back to the sailing wars with a flourish in 1958, when the America's Cup was revived in 12-Meters, and almost won the defender's berth in a dramatic battle with a new Stephens creation, *Columbia. Vim* didn't quite do it, and she was then sold to Australia, making possible the first challenge for the Cup from that far off land by acting as a trial horse for their new boats. All this was under new ownership, but somehow, Mike Vanderbilt seemed to be watching over her with a special glint in his eye, and she remained the last of the many great yachts in the Vanderbilt tradition.

The original *Corsair*—the name came with her secondhand

5

The Morgans

Of all the names that lent an aura of glamor to yachting in its most glamorous era, the heyday of the big steam yachts, that of Morgan must rank at the top. The four Morgan *Corsairs* were premium fixtures of the yachting scene from 1882 to 1939, and they were the absolute epitome of the word "yacht" to yachtsmen and the general public alike. Although their length ranged from 185 to 343 feet, they all had the same look—a graceful, glossy black hull, clipper bow and bowsprit, and raking buff stack.

Anyone who saw a *Corsair* steaming down the Hudson in the 1880s, ranging the Riviera and the Adriatic in the years just before World War I or looming hugely over the spectator fleet at a Yale-Harvard crew regatta, would know that she was a *Corsair* and that they had seen yachting at its finest.

And then there was J. Pierpont Morgan's famous statement, which, as we have seen, was made to a newly rich oil entrepreneur named Henry Clay Pierce. His pronouncement that "you have no right to own a yacht if you have to ask that question"—that is, how much it would cost—has become the stock cliché in the field, used in his lead paragraph by every writer assigned to do a feature on boats and yachting. Cliché or not, it was an apt remark at the time, though it was obviously not said with today's outboard runabouts, cabin cruisers and small auxiliaries in mind. It was said of the world of the Astors, Vanderbilts, Goulds, Bennetts, Lorillards and other newly rich nineteenth-century industrialists who spared no expense to make their yachts status symbols of their own success.

Although the name *Corsair* became one of the enduring ones of the field, and there were many reformers of the New Deal stripe who felt it had a special aptness during the dark days of the 1930s, when Wall Street was coming under the most severe attacks in its history, it came into the family with no special significance. It was simply the name of the yacht that J. Pierpont Morgan bought in 1882, when he decided to join the fraternity. Built in 1880 by William Cramp and Sons in Philadelphia, she was a sistership of George Osgood's *Stranger*, the yacht that had astounded Newport society by transporting Osgood from the Rhode Island resort to New York between breakfast and dinner. These vessels were 185′ x 23′ x 9′3½″ with twin screw engines of 760 hp. each, capable of over 15 knots.

The sistership had been offered to Morgan soon after she was built, but he did not make the decision to buy her until the summer of 1882, when he had a pleasant time in England being entertained aboard several yachts. He cabled his office to buy *Corsair*, and the sleek, rakish vessel was there to meet him when he came home by ocean liner in the early fall. She took him right from the steamship pier to the family estate at Cragston in Highland Falls, N.Y., on the Hudson River near West Point. When his wife and children arrived later in the fall by ship, *Corsair* was there to meet them too. Morgan joined the New York Yacht Club that year to begin the family's long and influential connection with that institution.

Corsair was soon outbuilt. Cramp turned out Jay Gould's 248-foot *Atalanta* in 1883, the first *Nourmahal*, a 232-footer, appeared in 1884, and the "I've-got-a-bigger-yacht-than-you-have" race was on in earnest. Morgan made do with his vessel until 1891, when the increasing size of his family, and of the yachts of other industrialists, led him to order a new *Corsair*. The name was to remain the same, and she was to have the same general appearance. In fact, naval architect J. Frederick Tams, who had been called in to discuss the new boat, ventured to criticize *Corsair I* and thought he had lost the assignment when Morgan, an imposing figure of a man with walrus moustache and great black eyebrows, fixed a cold stare on him. The subject was quickly dropped, but Tams did get the job and was given a book of blank checks and told to get the job done on his own without bothering Morgan again.

The new boat was to be 241 feet long, a size that could still maneuver in the Hudson off Cragston, with generally more room aboard, and about five knots more speed than *Corsair I*. She soon became a familiar fixture on the New York scene. Morgan used her frequently for business conferences, and she was usually anchored near the Jersey side of the Hudson across from the New York Yacht Club's Thirty-fifth Street landing. To get away from the new-fangled telephone, Morgan would take a business group aboard, and the future course of many a steel company or railroad was settled as *Corsair* steamed along the Palisades or turned her bow seaward through the Narrows to the cooling breezes off Sandy Hook.

Politicians, too, were entertained aboard, including President Grover Cleveland. During one financial crisis, a meeting between Morgan and Cleveland would have caused too much comment in the press. Nevertheless, they were able to effect a secret marine rendezvous to hold a discussion without the press finding out. Cleveland boarded the yacht *Oneida*, belonging to Commodore Benedict of Seawanhaka Corinthian Yacht Club on which he was a frequent social guest, at his summer home on Buzzards Bay, and she steamed westward down the bay and across Block Island Sound. In a cove on Gardiner's Island, a private preserve in the bay between the two points forming the "fish's tail" of Long Island, *Corsair* was waiting. *Oneida* came in, anchored nearby, and Morgan went aboard for a private chat with Cleveland. On the eve of President McKinley's election, Mark Hanna, the "king maker" from Ohio who was McKinley's campaign manager, was a visitor aboard *Corsair*, and royalty also trod her teak decks when they visited the United States.

Corsair II was working out well, and Morgan was very much at home with her. She was also a family yacht, used frequently for summer cruises, and she was of course one of the features of the

J. P. Morgan

annual New York Yacht Club cruise and of the spectator fleet at America's Cup Races. All this wasn't to last very long, however, as the war with Spain suddenly erupted. The United States found itself in it with almost no Navy, and an emergency program was instituted to commandeer private yachts for conversion as gunboats. As one of the best built yachts in the country, *Corsair* was soon singled out. Morgan was vexed at the thought, but finally submitted to pressure, and the gleaming black hull soon disappeared behind a coat of gray paint. The government paid $225,000 for her and re-named her U.S.S. *Gloucester* after stripping her of her luxury fittings and putting suitable armament on her.

At the Battle of Santiago, she earned her keep by taking on the Spanish torpedo boats *Furor* and *Pluton*. One ended up burning on the beach, and the other sank. Morgan fretted through one summer on a chartered yacht and then decided to order a new *Corsair* rather than wait for the *Gloucester* to be decommissioned. As it turned out, she stayed on duty through World War I and finally was sunk in 1919 when she hit a reef in the Gulf of Mexico while engaged in charting the area. Salvaged, she was eventually sold to a Greek owner.

Again, the new *Corsair* was to have the overall look of her predecessors, though she was to be bigger. As her designer, Morgan chose John Beavor-Webb, an Englishman who had done the designs for the America's Cup challengers *Genesta* and *Galatea* and then settled in the United States and became a citizen. There was to be the "feel" of being aboard the old *Corsair* to the extent that the pattern for the carpets was to be the same. When it was found that the pattern was no longer available, it was set up again at the factory so that the carpets of the new yacht would match the old ones. In general, accommodations on the *Corsairs* were comfortable in the extreme, with touches of elegance in the china and service, but they were not as showy as on some lesser yachts, and the overall accent was on handsome utility. She had six staterooms in her owner's quarters, a large library the width of the hull and lounges in her two deckhouses.

Corsair III was impressively big at 304' x 33'6" x 15'6" and 252' on the waterline, but the general feeling was still one of slender grace. Clinton Crane, who designed many steam yachts himself, paid tribute to Beavor-Webb's creation in his memoirs as "the handsomest steam yacht ever built," and there were many more who agreed with this opinion.

There was a wonderful symmetry to her. She had a bold, beautifully curved sheer, with gilded figurehead and trailboards to set it off, and her long, low deckhouses were perfectly in proportion to her hull, masts and stack. The slender 100-foot masts and traditional buff stack raked at just the right angle to complement the sheer and long graceful overhangs of the clipper bow and counter stern of a hull that would have looked at home under a cloud of square-rigged canvas.

She was built by T. S. Marvell and Sons in Newburgh, N.Y., near Cragston, and her engine and boilers came from W. A. Fletcher and Co. of Hoboken, N.J.

One reason Morgan wanted his own yacht for the year 1899 was that he had been elected Commodore of the New York Yacht Club and did not want a chartered flagship. At her commissioning, the new *Corsair* started right out, therefore, as queen of the fleet, and after his two terms as Commodore were over, she remained that unofficially for the rest of her career. There was pride in every inch of *Corsair*, in the bearing of her crew of fifty-five officers and men, and in the way they kept her. She had special touches that set her apart, such as the maple paneling of the upper engine housing, where it extended into the main deckhouse. Her main-engine cylinders were also lagged in maple, and all of this, including an unusual amount of engine-room brightwork in the railings, paneling and trim, was maintained and polished to mirror brightness.

Happy to be on his own vessel again, Morgan led the Yacht Club cruise proudly that summer, and found out, also, some of the extra financial burdens of having to do a Commodore's entertaining. In his business life, *Corsair* was almost in daily use. With the family at Cragston, she would take him there on a Friday evening and weekends would be spent there, both ashore and aboard the yacht. Sunday evening, *Corsair's* lean bow would head downstream, her farewell whistle blast echoing away between the steep crags of the Highlands of the Hudson. In the morning, she would be anchored off Thirty-fifth Street, where Morgan, now called The Commodore by most of

The second *Corsair*

More views of the second *Corsair*

his associates, would eat an amazingly hearty breakfast of several courses before taking the launch ashore to the office. On week nights, *Corsair* often threaded through the East River traffic to Great Neck at the western end of Long Island Sound, where friends who lived there would be entertained aboard. During this period, there was almost constant entertaining, and the Commodore did more than his share as an eater and drinker of gargantuan capacity. A group of friends who were often aboard with him were known as the Corsair Club. Beavor-Webb was one of them, along with Morgan's personal physician, Dr. Markoe, and titled visitors from abroad were frequently entertained as well.

Despite his bulk and disinclination to exercise for the sake of it, Morgan was a man of great physical strength. This was demonstrated in spectacular fashion once when *Corsair* took him out to the pilot station off Sandy Hook to meet the liner *Oceanic* on which his family was returning from Europe. The launch took him from the yacht to the liner, where a pilot's ladder was dangling down the sheer cliff of the ship's side. Without waiting to check whether this was the best way aboard, the Commodore, in formal garb and top hat, seized the swaying ladder and started climbing it, cigar clenched in his teeth, as it lurched and bounced against the rough steel plates of the ship's side. It was a long rugged climb to the rail as the ship's company, and those on the yacht, watched in considerable suspense. Had he dropped off, it would have been extremely difficult to recover him, but, sweating profusely, he finally made it, and, swinging over the rail unassisted, merely said "Where is Mrs. Morgan?" to the nearest steward and set off to find her, leaving everyone else limp and breathless.

In 1902 he took *Corsair* to Europe and began a routine, that was to last until his death in 1913, of long cruises in the Mediterranean and Aegean, along with visits to Northern European ports. After a crossing or two in the yacht, he decided that this was too rough for comfort, and he would send *Corsair* abroad, following by liner to board her for the cruising. In almost every country, he visited with the royal families. He had an audience with the Pope, and many royal figures were entertained on board.

His son, J. P., Jr. who was generally known as Jack to his family and intimates, had followed his father in business in The House of Morgan investment bank, and also in his interest in yachting, and when J. Pierpont died in 1913, Jack took over *Corsair* and maintained the same traditions and operations, though his family home was in Glen Cove, L. I., instead of up the Hudson. The way of life that had fostered these traditions was soon shattered, however, by the gathering storm in Europe.

It was during the New York Yacht Club cruise of 1914 that word came of the outbreak of war. An all-night meeting of owners on *Corsair* brought the decision to cancel the rest of the cruise. Whether these owners also knew that a whole way of life was being canceled is hard to say, but the climate in which the big yachts were operated until that summer was never to return in exactly the same way.

When the United States entered the war, the Navy acquired the Morgans' yacht, as it had in 1898, but this time it was a one-dollar deal. She was taken to the Fletcher plant in Hoboken, where her yachty paneling and fittings were stripped, and she was fitted with depth charges, Y-guns and armament. Bunk space was added for 12 officers and 122 men. This time she kept her name, and her professional captain under Morgan, William B. Porter, was made her exec as a Lieutenant Commander. Commander Theodore A. Kittenger, an Annapolis graduate, was her commanding officer until Porter succeeded him in 1918.

Her crew was made up mostly of young reserves from Princeton, and by June 14, 1917, she was off on her first convoy as one of its ten escorts, bound for St. Nazaire, France. Here she joined a number of other yachts that had also been converted, and instead of gathering in Newport or Marion for the New York Yacht Club cruise that summer, in gray paint they operated on the Breton patrol out of Brest. *Corsair* was almost continuously on convoy duty and participated in several rescues of crews of torpedoed ships. In December 1917, she was caught in one of the worst storms in the history of the stormy Bay of Biscay and had to limp south to Lisbon, unable to make headway into a French port. It took six weeks to repair the damage.

She ended her Navy duty as flagship for Admiral Sims in Queens-town, Ireland, and finally came home, just a month short of two years after her departure, to be decommissioned. The Fletcher Yard was given her extensive refit, and Morgan ended up paying much of the cost, as it far exceeded Navy estimates. Her deckhouse was altered and the dining saloon moved to it, making more room for the crew's quarters below. She was also refitted for oil fuel, with water tube boilers, and the shine and polish were restored to her paint and brass.

It was just in time, as once again she was to be flagship of the New York Yacht Club, twenty-one years after her initial stint. Jack Morgan was Commodore in 1920, and *Corsair* resumed her role as queen of them all, even though for the next ten years, there was a last spasm of building great yachts. Anything went in the 20s, and as the stock market soared, millionaires went back to the building race, turning out giant after giant. Not the biggest any more, *Corsair* was still the handsomest by almost general agreement, but, as the mad 20s soared to a climax, Morgan decided to move up the scale too.

In January 1929, he placed an order with the firm of H. J. Gielow, Inc. in New York to design *Corsair IV*. Henry Gielow himself, who had designed many of the largest luxury yachts of the era, had died in 1925, but the firm was still going strong, and Morgan asked for a 343-footer, still to be a steam yacht, though oil-fired. She was to be the largest pleasure craft ever built in this country, and the order to build her was given to Bath Iron Works in Maine. Joseph Mac-Donald, who headed the Gielow organization, had a working agreement with Bath, and in addition to placing the order for *Corsair*, a $2,500,000 one, on July 9, 1929 he signed to build five identical 190-foot yachts on speculation. It took Gielow and the builders an entire decade to unload those five $500,000 boats, whose keels had just been laid when the stock market collapsed on October 24, 1929, and only four of them went as yachts. The fifth finally was taken by the Navy in 1941. *Corsair IV* was delivered, however, and *Corsair III* went back into government service for the final time.

Morgan did not want to sell the fine old vessel, but she still had many useful years in her, so she went to The Coast and Geodetic Sur-

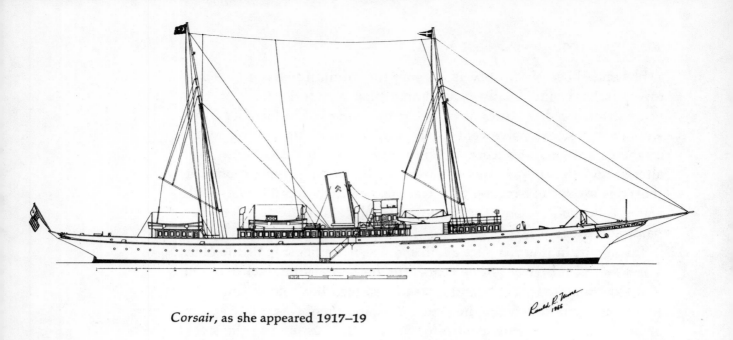

Corsair, as she appeared 1917–19

Corsair, the lines from her docking plan

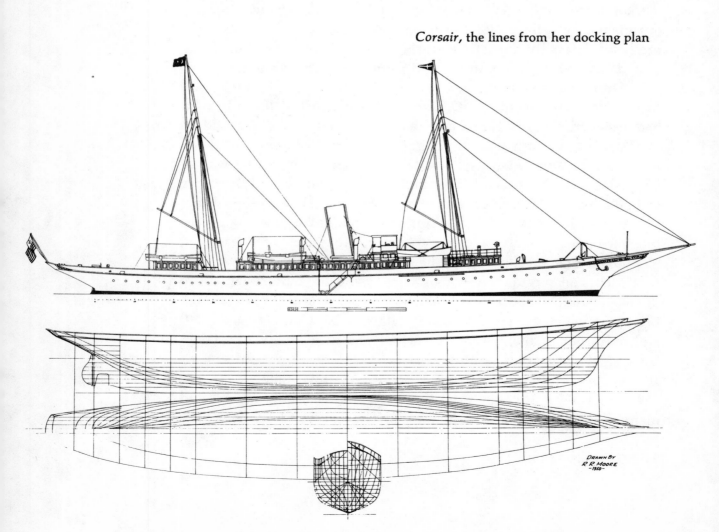

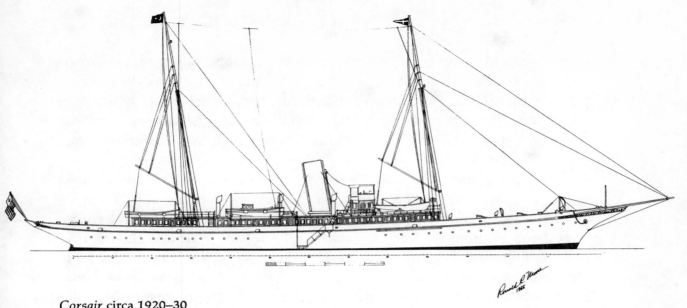

Corsair circa 1920–30

Oceanographer ex *Corsair*, as in the U.S. Navy 1942–44

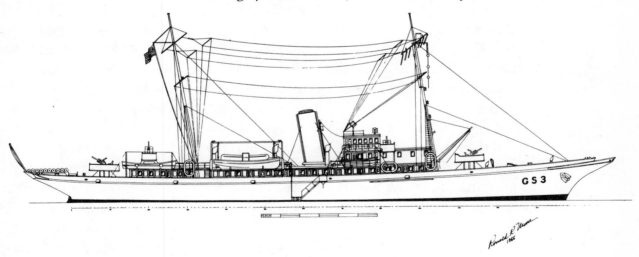

Various stages of the third *Corsair*. Designed by John Beavor-Webb in 1899, she was 304 in length overall, 252 feet at the waterline and 33.5 feet in beam. She was decommissioned and broken up in 1944.

vey as *Oceanographer*. Still yacht-like in appearance, though stripped of the fancier luxury trappings, she did survey work off the East Coast. New techniques developed on her helped locate many previously uncharted shoals and canyons in the offshore area, and she was hard at it off the Carolina Coast eleven years later on Pearl Harbor Day.

Once again the Navy wanted her, as there was desperate need for patrol boats off the coast in the early days of the war. With U-boats ranging at will right into the mouths of harbors and rivers, and burning oil from torpedoings lacing the beaches, almost anything that floated, even an 1899 luxury yacht, looked like help. *Oceanographer* (almost everyone still referred to her as *Corsair*) was ordered to a small shipyard the Navy had taken over in Norfolk, Va., for conversion once more to a gunboat. It so happens that the author was assigned to her on temporary duty as officer-in-charge of a skeleton Navy crew that was working on her to get her ready for conversion, and a first glimpse of her against the cluttered background of the yard on the Elizabeth River revealed the still handsome sheer and raked stack as clear trademarks despite all that was being done to her. The desperate need of the Navy could be told in one glance around the yard. The other two vessels there, also being fitted out for patrol duty in a crash program, were the 1898 gunboat *Dubuque*, and, most modern of the trio, one of Henry Ford's Eagle boats from World War I. Actually, new subchasers were beginning to come out in droves, and by the time *Corsair's* refit was finished, the worst crisis was over.

An inventory tour of *Oceanographer* revealed that she still had some yacht-like features. A storekeeper who had come from the back mountains of Kentucky, and had never been on anything that floated before, was having a difficult time with nautical terminology as we checked off items. Each time he was told it was a "ladder" instead of a "staircase," a "bulkhead" instead of a "wall" or a "deck" instead of a "floor," he would shake his head and groan, but his eyes lit up when we went into the grand saloon and were confronted by a handsome paneled fireplace. With a laugh of triumph he said, "Bet you cain't tell me no boat name fo' a fah-place."

The third *Corsair*

J. P. Morgan and his son Junius Morgan

Later, in what had once been the owner's quarters, we shoved open the door of a bathroom ("head," the storekeeper had to be told) to find a brawny machinist's mate, covered with grime, washing up at an ornate marble basin and eying himself in a large, gilt-edged mirror. Taking one look and rolling his eyes skyward, the storekeeper pulled the door shut as he murmured "Shades of J. P. Morgan!"

Oceanographer, though armed and ready for combat, was still needed for survey work in some of the strange areas the Navy was entering for the first time in history, and she ended up in such diverse regions as the Aleutians and the Southwest Pacific. Often working by herself in waters exposed to enemy action, she was never attacked. She surveyed The Solomons, The New Hebrides, Bougainville and New Caledonia, working almost endlessly, but finally the years began to tell. In August 1944 she was ordered back to Long Beach, Calif., for overhaul, but an examination revealed that the forty-five years had taken their toll and that repairs would not be worth it. In accordance with Morgan's deed of gift back in 1930, which specified that she was to be broken and not sold when she had outlived her usefulness, that was her eventual fate. She was decommissioned on September 21, 1944.

Her successor did not have as long, varied and productive a life. By the time she was delivered in 1930, she had become a symbol that was to hurt Morgan in subsequent Congressional investigations of Wall Street dealings. In the depths of the Depression, the largest yacht ever built in the country was not an object to make the man selling the apples on the corner happy with the state of affairs in the country.

Strictly as a vessel, forgetting any symbolic resentment she might have aroused, she was a really big ship compared to her predecessors. Though only 40 feet longer, she had much more bulk and cubic space. Still, she retained the black hull, the clipper bow, the bowsprit, and the raked funnel and masts of all the *Corsairs*, and there was no mistaking the line of descent. These features combined to spell Morgan and *Corsair*, and she stood out even more boldly as her contemporaries began to go out of commission.

Through the dark days of 1931-33, she was one of the few big yachts operating in this country, and in 1934 she was taken on a major voyage, a cruise through the West Indies and Panama Canal to the Galapagos Islands off Ecuador in the Pacific. She made an impressive sight in such out-of-the-way harbors as St. Kitts in the Leewards and in the rocky, barren coves of the Galapagos.

Even for the Morgans, mid-Depression pressures became too much. J. P. Morgan didn't make enough to have to pay any income tax in one year, and *Corsair* was finally laid up for the 1935 yachting season. With things picking up in the late 30s, she was back in commission again after the one-year lay-up, and she was again the major feature of the accompanying fleet of the New York Yacht Club cruises and of the spectator fleet at the 1937 America's Cup Races. She loomed as large as the excursion steamers lining the course, and one of the few yachts to approach her in size was *Philante*, the modern, rakish yacht of T. O. M. Sopwith, skipper of the challenging *Endeavour II*.

The summer of 1939 was the last for *Corsair* on the American scene. At the Yale-Harvard crew race in New London, she bulked over the spectator fleet, anchored along the course on the Thames River, like a large Mother Superior among children on a playground. A giant Harvard banner was suspended between her tall masts, bigger than the sail area of many of the small auxiliaries moored near her, and she was the dominant feature of a scene that was not to be repeated with the same elements.

That September, World War II broke the last remaining patterns of an era that the Depression had already ended, and *Corsair* went to the British Navy, again for one dollar, to serve as a gunboat.

Her eventual end was a sad one, as her postwar role was conversion to a cruise liner to run from Southern California to Acapulco. On her maiden voyage, she was stranded on the rocky shore near that Mexican port and ended up as scrap salvage.

The Morgan family continued very active in the sport on a different scale. Jack Morgan's son Henry S. Morgan concentrated on sail, with a lovely 62-foot ocean racing sloop named *Djinn*. He followed his father and grandfather as Commodore of the New York

The last *Corsair* after World War II at City Island, N.Y.

Yacht Club and headed its influential America's Cup Committee during the 12-Meter era. *Djinn*, long a boat to beat in major East Coast events and New York Yacht Club cruise runs, survived a dramatic knockdown in the 1960 Bermuda Race, when a freak squall caught her aback under genoa and main and threw her over on her beam ends on the opposite tack. Her crew, tossed around like laundry in an automatic washer, recovered without serious injury, although several were thrown out of their bunks and completely across the cabin, and only safety harnesses kept the men on deck from being swept away. Several years later, she was replaced by a Sparkman and Stephens motorsailer of the same size and name. Operated with a paid crew of two, comfortable, able and handsome, she represented, as a premium yacht of the 1960s, a dramatic contrast to the departed tradition of the sleek black *Corsairs*.

Part II

THE GOLDEN AGE

Vanadis—her delivery voyage was a near disaster

6

The Height of Luxury

The Vanderbilts and Morgans didn't hold stage center in the yachting world by themselves, although their names were better known to the general public and lived longer as household synonyms for wealth and social position. Other families whose names bring instant associations of great wealth, such as Rockefeller, Mellon and duPont, have been associated with the sport in varying ways, but not with showpiece *Corsairs*, *North Stars* and *Alvas*. The Astors, though not as prolifically active, kept the name *Nourmahal* alive for several generations.

By 1900, however, with new fortunes well-established in railroads, oil, steel and various branches of manufacture, there were many new millionaires ready to join the "club" of luxury yacht owners. In that year, Anthony J. Drexel of Philadelphia was quoted as saying that there were only three men in the world who could afford to run his yacht *Margarita*, which had ninety-three in her crew. Her carpeting had cost £3 a yard in England, and part of her original decor was a garden with real roses growing over trellises. The sea air was not a good atmosphere for the plants, however, and they died easily, so Drexel had rubber roses put up instead. These were also a failure, however, because the colors ran.

There were many such touches in the details of the yachts that proliferated in the early twentieth century. The *Flying Cloud* had a live cow aboard as fresh milk supply, but this created a nuisance of flies, so the crew was paid a bounty for killing, and turning in for head count, as many flies as they could.

The Astors had *Nourmahal's* crew eating off fine tablecloths in the crew's mess, prompting a visitor to shake his head and remark "Sailors with tablecloths— what would Nelson have said?" On the yacht of tin-plate heir Leeds, pet monkeys were a feature, and, when one of them got off his chain and into the cabin of a guest known for his heavy drinking, a quick cure was supposedly effected.

Nicholas Brown, the Rhode Island millionaire, once tipped a crew $2,000 after a pleasant weekend on a friend's yacht, and sent a $5,000 tip to the supervisor of construction of a yacht he was having built in England. Another American millionaire with a cavalier approach to cash was M. Bayard Brown, who became an eccentric recluse aboard his *Valfreya* on a mooring off Brightlingsea in England. Steam was kept up at all times, although she never once left her mooring, and Brown remained shut in his cabin for days on end. With the boat deteriorating around him, he would occasionally appear on deck and throw handfuls of money overboard. When the Maharajah of Nawanger bought *Valfreya* after Brown's death in 1927 and renamed her *Star of India*, the crew's quarters had to be rebuilt with separate forecastles and eating facilities for the different castes of Indians in the crew.

Publisher Joseph Pulitzer, who was almost totally blind and also very sensitive to noise, built the handsome 250-foot *Liberty* in 1908 and spent much of his time on her "cruising to nowhere" offshore in the Atlantic, keeping in touch with his office by wireless. Because of his poor eyesight, her passenger quarters had no sharp projections of any kind, and he also had soundproofed bulkheads installed. To reduce the noise level, no work was permitted aboard except at specified hours, as the muffled sound of a hammer banging far below decks could send Pulitzer into a towering rage.

In 1907 there were eight yachts over 300 feet long on the New York Yacht Club roster. The largest was James Gordon Bennett's *Lysistrata* at 314 feet. All the big yachts were not in the New York

Hugh Chisholm's *Aras* eventually became the presidential yacht *Williamsburgh*

Venetia and owner's stateroom

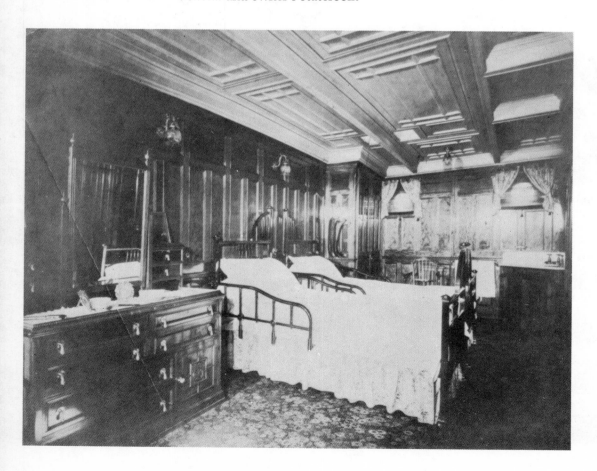

Aztec

The owner's stateroom

The music room

Yacht Club however. Occasionally a millionaire who was not able to get along with his fellow nabobs was blackballed, and this sometimes led to the founding of other clubs. Jay Gould, a crusty loner who was at odds with "the establishment" and was not taken in to the New York Yacht Club, founded American Yacht Club at Rye, N.Y., in a fit of "I'll show 'em" and several other now prestigious clubs owe their founding to similar situations.

The last year before World War I brought the luxury yacht era to its peak, but the luxury yacht was revived with new touches after the wartime break. Some of the old cast of characters was still active, but there was new money, in new places, and the big yachts were no longer confined to the Northeastern part of the country. Horace E. Dodge was one of the first new automobile millionaires to become a yachtsman, building *Nokomis*, a 243-footer with all the usual appointments, a music room 20 x 6 x 24 feet, 7 small boats, and a cruising range of 9,000 miles at 16.5 knots.

Lyndonia, a 240-footer built in 1920 for publisher Cyrus H. K. Curtis had period rooms in various styles. Writing in *Yachting* in July 1920 in an article entitled "How the Millionaire Does It," George W. Sutton, Jr., described this "yacht of the year."

"The stateroom of Mr. and Mrs. Curtis looks no more like a part of a boat than would any tastefully decorated 19 by 16 bedroom in a fine residence. It is exactly that. With its beautiful twin beds, settee, dressing table and mirrors, and its delicately formed electric light fixtures, it is a perfect work of the Adam period. The original plan was to have the stateroom represent the Louis XVI Period, but it was changed. The carpet in this room was especially woven for the occasion. The dining room might have been transplanted from the St. Regis. It is in the Jacobean Period and is 24 feet 3 inches by 16 feet 6 inches, with silken curtains, and a particularly artistic ceiling. The saloon, in which one can loaf most effetely, is in the simple treatment of the William and Mary Period, with walnut predominating in the settees, sofas, lounges and other panaceas for fatigue. It is 25 feet long and 17 feet wide, with plate glass windows and elab-

Niagara

The music room

Cyprus was a typical Cox and Stevens creation

The smoking room

The grand saloon

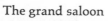

The dining room

orate electric candelabra. The Tudor Epoch is immortalized in the smoking room. Here the general tone is grey, and one finds an oak desk, harmonious paneling, and leather armchairs to ease one's bones.

"The other day I dined in what is supposed to be one of the most exquisitely furnished rooms in the world. It is in a restaurant which was formerly a gambling house maintained by an internationally known gentleman, whose pleasure it was to teach Casino, Old Maid, Hearts and Double Canfield to the rich and their sons (usually at different times). It was furnished, I should say, in the Liberal Period, when polished mahogany was a nickel a foot and Italian marble was given away. I received something of the same impression when wandering through *Lyndonia's* six guest rooms. The difference is that, on *Lyndonia*, the builders were thinking of such material things as comfort, convenience and good taste instead of simply lavish outlay. The rooms are gems—in the American Colonial and Eighteenth Century Periods—with slumber inducing twin beds and all the comforts of a modest home—on Fifth Avenue.

"For the ablutionary exercises of the owner and his guests, there are seven tiled bathrooms, any one of which is 'way ahead of the historic baths of the famous Pompeiian gentleman.'"

Pianos, pipe organs and fully-equipped music rooms were a standard feature on most of the big yachts. On *Lounger IV*, owned by typewriter tycoon James Hammond, there was also a special touch in the master stateroom. As he lay on his bed—not bunk—Hammond could work a lever beside it that raised the bed enough for him to look out of the porthole without getting up. There is another apocryphal story about movable beds that supposedly came to light when the yacht of a famous womanizing playboy was taken over by the Navy in World War II. The young commanding officer moved into the master stateroom and began playing around with various buzzers and buttons on the bulkhead to see what their functions were. Suddenly, to his surprise, the bulkhead next to the bed rolled up, and the officer in the next cabin was tumbled through the opening from his own bed onto the big double one in the master stateroom.

The music room of Max Fleischman's *Haida* was likened to a reception room at Buckingham Palace by *Yachting*, and another yacht's appointments were called similar to an old world feudal estate. More practically, diesel engines began to replace steam on all but the very largest yachts, reducing the size of crew needed, and doing away with the messy business of coaling, soot on deck, and the awareness, though it never seemed to nag much at the conscience of any owners or passengers, of the grimy black gang shoveling coal into the stokeholes in the depths of the vessel.

British yacht broker Herbert E. Julyan wrote his memoirs of selling luxury yachts to famous customers in a book called *Sixty Years of Yachts* and described one of his most difficult sales as that of *Ronen*, the 320-foot yacht of Lord Inchcape. When she went on the market in the early 1930s, the King of Roumania was interested in her and a sale appeared imminent when a cable was received from the American brokerage firm of Cox and Stevens offering £100,000, against the King's offer of £63,000, on behalf of an anonymous bidder.

Cox and Stevens was informed that the King had first refusal but that this option would run out at a meeting at a certain time in Julyan's office. The King's representative failed to show, and the deal with the mysterious American was closed by cable. Not until much later did Julyan find out that the buyer was Howard Hughes. He then wrote and asked Hughes when he would like to see his new purchase and the answer was "When I have time."

Six weeks later, with no advance warning, Hughes showed up at Falmouth, where the yacht was lying, and was naturally stopped by the watchman. "It's okay," said Hughes. "I'm the owner."

Julyan had his difficulties dealing with the eccentric new owner. After long periods of silence, Hughes would suddenly demand all sorts of attention and expected Julyan to drop everything else and come when called. Once he was summoned after lunch to find Hughes having breakfast in his hotel room and sending a boiled egg back ten times before it was done the way he wanted.

Hughes renamed the yacht *Southern Cross* and eventually took her

A newer *Vanadis* was built in Kiel in 1924

Lyndonia

to California, where she lay at anchor off Santa Barbara much of the time. She had been the largest yacht in Europe, and now she was the largest on the West Coast. Eventually she was sold to Axel Wenner-Gren, the Swedish millionaire, who started on a world cruise in her but was interrupted by the outbreak of World War II. *Southern Cross* rescued 500 passengers from the torpedoed liner *Athenia* on her way across the Atlantic then was sold into government service because of the war when she reached Panama.

The age of the big yacht was fully at an end by this time. In 1929, at the height of the optimism of the 1920s, J. P. Morgan had started his last *Corsair* at Bath Iron Works, and one other great name from the early days of luxury yachts received its last extension when Vincent Astor built a new *Nourmahal* in 1928. His ancestor John Jacob, who came from Waldorff, Germany, to New York as a lad of twenty in 1783, and, on the basis of an acquaintance with a fur trapper made on shipboard coming over, built a giant fur trading business that gave him the largest American fortune, $30,000,000, when he died in 1848, was socially established before many of the men who became famous yachtsmen made their fortunes, but he had not become involved with yachting in any way. It was John Jacob his grandson, sometimes known as "the landlord of New York" because of the family's extensive real estate holdings, who built the first *Nourmahal* (which means "light of the harem").

Vincent Astor, who didn't use his first name of William, built one *Nourmahal* in 1921, when he was thirty, and cruised in her extensively. Like Vanderbilt's *Ara*, she was armed with guns to guard against pirates in lonely waters.

The last *Nourmahal* was a 263-foot diesel yacht built for what now seems the incredible price of $600,000 (it would be many times that today) at the Krupp Works in Germany. Designed by Theodore Ferris of Cox and Stevens, she did not have the traditional clipper bow, a hangover from sailing ship days, that so many of the fanciest yachts sported. Her stem was plumb, giving her the look of a compact ocean liner, and her equipment was, of course, the most modern and complete that could be installed at the time.

Nourmahal remained in the public eye during the 1930s in a very special way, as Franklin Delano Roosevelt often was a guest aboard her for short cruises away from the pressures of Washington. There was a measure of irony in his presence on this arrant symbol of rugged individualism and unfettered capitalism while his legislative program was bringing about the social reforms and tax programs that spelled the end of this sort of thing.

Once, jokingly, looking around *Nourmahal*, he said to Astor that he guessed he would have to raise the taxes on the rich some more. The remark no doubt held little humor for Astor, but it was prophetic concerning the end of one era in yachting.

Before the era died, however, it produced some fascinating vessels.

Coronet

Colonel John Jacob Astor

The *Nourmahal* of the 1890s

Nourmahal of the 1920s

The Dodges' *Delphine*

A luxury stateroom of the 1920s with fewer frills and simple decor

Philante's lounge

T. O. M. Sopwith's *Endeavours*, J-boat challengers for the America's Cup, were accompanied by his *Philante*, one of the largest and most luxurious yachts of the 1930s

The large drawing room of *Philante*

Philante's dining saloon

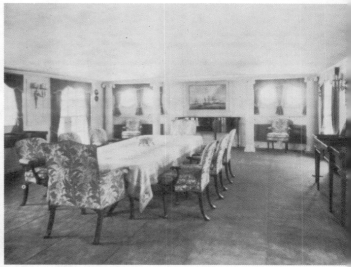

Southern Cross, the 338-foot yacht Howard Hughes bought sight unseen

The presidential yacht
Mayflower

Henry Manville's 226-foot *Hi-Esmaro* was one of the major yachts from
Henry Gielow

Opposite: *Caroline* on her builder's trials

Caroline's grand saloon

Aloha at anchor

7

Aloha

Once, while twilight of an evening in late June lingered and glim-
mered over the wake churned by the paddles of the Fall River Line
steamer *Priscilla* as she steamed eastward on Long Island Sound, the
author, bound for a summer at Nantucket, Mass., in the mid-20s,
chanced to see one of the memorable spectacles of the era.

Ahead of us, a splotch of white flickered against the gathering
darkness. Coastal schooners were still thick along that route, and
it was a common sight to come up on them as they plodded their
way through the evening calm, grayish sails hanging slack in the
zephyrs. This splotch diffused and grew bigger, however, spreading
higher and whiter against the wall of night, until a pattern of square-
rigged sails could be seen. Swiftly *Priscilla* overtook the vessel as the
sails loomed higher, and suddenly her black hull and rigging pattern
firmed in the pale light. We left her on the port hand, and as she fell
back on the quarter, the ghostly white of her sails changed to sharp
silhouettes. There, against the glow remaining in the northwest sky,
was the starkly outlined tracery of the rigging and sails of a graceful
bark. For a moment she stood bold against the horizon, and towered
into the night, a dramatic reminder of an era that had already gone
by. Fire from the departed sun tipped her upper yards and glinted
off some glossy patch of paint on her topsides, and then, with *Pris-*

cilla steadily chunk-chunking her way eastward, the vision faded astern into the murk of descending night and became nothing more than the wink of running lights dimming rapidly.

Someone along the rail murmured "*Aloha*" as the ship stood against the sunset, for that's what she was, the beautiful 202-foot bark Arthur Curtiss James had built as flagship of the New York Yacht Club in 1910. She was intended for a trip around the world, but World War I prevented it. James finally fulfilled his dream in 1921. She was one of the most romantic yachts ever built, a bridge between the age of square-riggers and the luxurious floating palaces of the early twentieth century. No one who saw her will ever forget her.

And a lot of people saw her. James was not a harbor sailor, content to sit on the fantail and have stewards serve drinks while he surveyed the surroundings. From young manhood on, he used his boats for real cruising. His first vessel, given to him by his father in 1893, was the 125-foot schooner *Coronet*, which he called ideal as a vessel for "a young man to learn about seamanship and navigation." He cruised her over 60,000 miles between the West Indies and the Gulf of St. Lawrence and on one passage to Japan and back.

In 1899 he had the first *Aloha* built, a 130-foot schooner which he termed "a splendid little vessel." All in northern latitudes, he cruised her for 152,560 miles in the next ten years with several visits to the Mediterranean and West Indies. Through all this voyaging, a dream of wider horizons had been in James's mind. He really couldn't say that he had done all the cruising he wanted to until he had gone around the world. Accounts of the nineteenth-century voyages of Sir Thomas Brassey's *Sunbeam* had fired his imagination as a youngster, and, while sailing the first *Aloha*, he continually planned ahead for what would be the consummation of the dream.

The new *Aloha* was to be the instrument, and she was planned and built expressly for this purpose. As a preliminary, he took her to the Mediterranean several times, and even into the Red Sea, but plans for the longer cruise had to be shelved as the world came closer and closer to war. With the United States finally in it, the lovely *Aloha* was taken over by the Navy for patrol duty but James got her back and re-fitted her in her former state of luxury.

Aloha under full sail

Finally, by September 1921, the long-deferred cruise could be started. The war was well out of the way, *Aloha* was ready, and James and his wife had collected a party of male and female friends to take the cruise with them, including a doctor, Karl Vogel, who wrote a book about the voyage. The dream that had begun in the 1890s was finally being lived out.

At 11:00 A.M. on September 15, as the ship's bell sounded and friends and relatives on the pier waved and shouted, lines were cast off from *Aloha's* berth in New York's East River. Her triple-expansion steam engines sent her down river with the tide, where her mast truck, 131 feet above the water, barely missed the Brooklyn Bridge, past the skyscrapers of the financial district, and out through The Narrows to the open sea. *Aloha*, whose home berth was in the East River, was a familiar harbor fixture, and the plans of her cruise were well enough known so that tugs, ferry boats and fireboats saluted her with whistles and streams of water in the traditional New York Harbor rite usually reserved for new arrivals, as she made her stately way seaward.

It was an exciting sendoff, and the first leg of the cruise, a nonstop passage to Panama, was one of the pleasantest of the whole circumnavigation. As the ship's company settled into life aboard and admired the fine-looking young men who had been signed on in her thirty-eight-man crew, the prevailing westerlies sent her barreling south along the Jersey Coast at 11 knots. The pleasant weather improved to really fine conditions as she surged into the warm waters of the Gulf Stream after two days, and the joy of being afloat was made complete the first night in the Stream by a full moon silvering across the waves.

She moved swiftly southward, passing within sight of Turks Island, east of the Bahamas, and through the Windward Passage into the Caribbean as the sun warmed and the sea turned ever bluer. For the passengers, there were fishing from the fantail, deck tennis, and even setting up exercises to victrola music. Dr. Vogel vaccinated the ship's company in preparation for exotic ports ahead, and the evenings were taken up with cards, reading aloud, conversation and concerts by Commodore James on the pianola in the main saloon. Dr.

Vogel mentions a particularly stirring rendition of the funeral march from *Götterdämmerung* as the highlight of one of the concerts, by "Jake," as he called the owner, which seems a strange selection for entertaining such a light-hearted gathering. The first book they read together was Stanley's life of Queen Victoria.

Aloha made it to Panama in thirteen days, where the guests went ashore for a round of golf before taking part in the exciting process of locking through from Atlantic to Pacific. The 98-foot power yacht *Speejacks*, the first yacht without sail to go all the way around the world, was in the Canal Zone at the same time on her way westward, and the two ships' companies compared notes. *Speejacks* was headed for Tahiti, and her owners had to arrange for a tow behind a steamship for this portion of the cruise, as she couldn't carry enough fuel on board for the 4,800-mile crossing.

Aloha was headed farther north, for the islands that inspired her name, and then to Japan, and although she had her magnificent spread of sail to move her along, she was forced to use her auxiliary engines here and for long portions of the whole circumnavigation, as she had very poor luck with wind, even in the areas of predicted Trades. At least she avoided any really serious bad weather. She made 23.7 miles on a ton of coal, so a lot of shoveling took place to make the voyage possible.

She steamed westward through the doldrums for several days and finally picked up the Trades on October 23, which raised everyone's spirits with one of the most exciting sails of the cruise, a 290-mile day to noon of the twenty-fourth. Four days later she arrived off Hilo only to find fog, of all unlikely things. The twenty-eight-day passage was the longest non-stop one of the whole cruise.

The islands provided a round of parties at both Hilo and Honolulu, where many of the first families were friends of *Aloha's* guests, and they went sightseeing at such divergent local attractions as a pineapple plantation and a leper colony. The visitors were amazed at the gaiety and good spirits of the inmates of the colony, and couldn't believe that the happy people they saw singing together were in the dramatically dire straits that the situation brought to their minds.

The James fortune had come from banking, mining and interests that were expanded from these bases, and at almost every stop there was someone with whom the Commodore had business connections. In addition, a family foundation and other philanthropies had backed institutions for providing education for the poor at home, and for bringing education to foreign areas that had never known it, and these affiliations also meant visits and conferences in many ports.

From Hawaii, *Aloha* sailed northwestward into winter on her way to Japan on a twenty-two-day passage. On this leg, those aboard were impressed more than at any other time by the vast loneliness of the ocean. For most of it, they never saw another ship, and even fish and birds were absent. Only the continuously gray, heaving waves were with the ship as she plowed steadily westward. Card games became more and more of a time-user as the days went by, and they played so much that one of the guests, at the end of the cruise, figured that they had played 600 rubbers, and that, since they were all of fairly equal skill at bridge, the scores had evened out. They held "championships" for each ocean, and a different person won each one of them. If they had played for money, no one would have been more than a few dollars ahead of anyone else at journey's end. As they neared Japan, the weather turned bleak and cold, and the guests were glad to get ashore when they hit Yokohama.

Although this was a yachting cruise, the guests were really along as travelers, not sailors, and each stop saw them taking off to do the things that any well-heeled tourists would do if they had come by ocean liner. There was much socializing in Tokyo with Americans and Europeans living there and with Japanese leaders, who were thoroughly impressed, and in fact astounded at the scope of the *Aloha* adventure. *Aloha's* party visited temples and shrines and were continuously busy in sightseeing and social engagements.

Everything had been so well arranged, and life aboard the bark was so pleasant and well ordered that there seems to have been very little friction among the company. In port they went their several ways in small groups, and, from time to time, others joined the guest list for short portions of the cruise.

Leaving Japan, *Aloha* made her way through the crowded Inland Sea, towering over the hundreds of sampans and small commercial

Much of her world voyage was under power

Bridge was a continuous pastime of *Aloha*'s world cruise guests

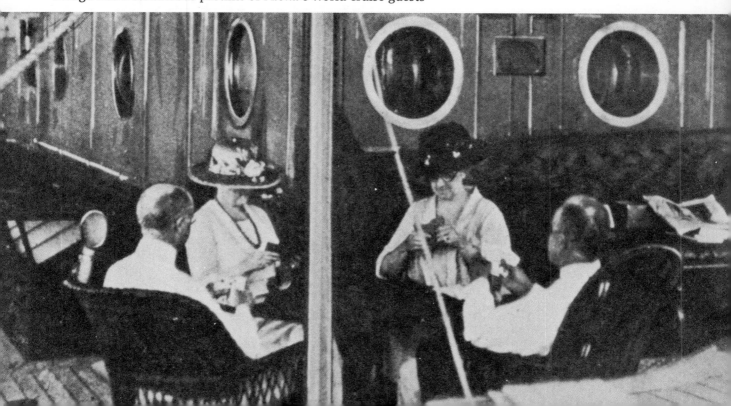

Commodore and Mrs. James receive guests in Hawaii

Aloha's party at the Pyramids

vessels that make this one of the world's busiest bodies of water.

The scenery was graceful, the marine life was colorful, and the ship herself, such a rare sight in these waters, was watched in awe as she threaded her way through the twisting, tide-swept channel of the Sea. It was here that she had one of the few misadventures of the whole circumnavigation. As she was steaming through a narrow cut between two islands, with a five-knot tidal current swirling under her, there was a sudden loud bang, as though she had hit something under water. It was soon discovered, however, that the noise had been a steering cable parting.

For a few moments, it looked like a crisis because of the narrow waters and swift current, but proper spares were readily available, repairs were made in a matter of minutes, and she continued on her serene way.

From the Inland Sea she exited via the Strait of Shimonoseki into the Sea of Japan and into one of the roughest portions of the cruise. A winter northwester was howling across the none-too-friendly body of water, kicking up a wicked sea, and all hands spent a few uncomfortable hours. Nothing serious happened, however, as she plowed her way toward Korea, and the port of Pusan.

The discomforts of the passage were soon forgotten in the landlocked picturesque and peaceful harbor, with a backdrop of mountains, whose shape seemed different in these exotic surroundings, so seldom seen by Western eyes, especially from the deck of a yacht.

The passengers traveled inland to Seoul and Mukden and were surprised at the comfort and modernity of the trains and hotels. Then they went across the frozen, barren plains of North China, a sea of dun-colored mud, to the excitement of Peking.

The Orient made a great impression on *Aloha's* passengers, but she also had a strong impact on it. Wherever she went, she was the object of much rubber-necking, and the ceremony of greeting visitors was constantly being played out on her quarterdeck. To help with language and local customs, a Japanese guide came aboard, and he became a vital part of the ship's company as he bustled about in friendly, helpful fashion.

Something of the exchange of impacts, and of the language problems that had to be overcome, comes through in quotes from local press comments on *Aloha's* visits to each port, as translated into English (of a sort) by the helpful guide, who knew his American friends would be interested. Dr. Vogel included them in his book with very little comment, as they really don't need it.

"The *Aloha* the graceful yacht of Mr. Arthur Curtiss James, who has been laying her beautiful body on the sea just in front of the Yokohama Y.C. is hurrying her departure to sail for Kobe tomorrow."

"In addition to important positions as director of Phelps Dodge Co. Mr. James is concerning widely into railways, banks and universities. Union Theological Seminary, N.Y. Library, Orphan Asylum and many navigation clubs are owing their good development to Mr. James. A large sum of capital in organization of school for education of niggers and American Indians in Hampton, a girls' technical school in Turkey, Laborers Hall in America are finding its resources entirely in the pocket of Mr. James."

"Mr. James is Trying a Brave Round World Trotting Crossing Pacific Ocean in Family Size Yacht.

"One of the greatest businessmen and at the same time a great monarch of charity in U.S.A. Mr. A. C. James and his consort arrived in Yokohama on his Auxiliary Yacht *Aloha* on the 30th escorted by a number of prominent business men and scholars. . . . He is conducting many navigation clubs, childrens asylums, libraries and Union Theological Seminary as a financial background or advising director . . . *Aloha* is an extremely luxurious boat accomplished with playrooms and bedrooms named after its color."

"Extremely Adventurous Round World Sightseeing. The great scheme of Mr. and Mrs. Arthur Curtiss James, Director of Amherst College, U.S.A. to cross Pacific Ocean on a graceful yacht was taking notice of all the world as a most adventurous round world trip in recent date. . . . *Aloha* is the name of the yacht in which they are sitting now and means God help me in

Hawaiian language. . . . The construction of yacht is extremely ingenious but is an extreme adventure to cross Pacific Ocean without use of steam engine and much more brave deeds to make round world trotting by the same. Mr. James has very clear brain and solved any hard problem in five minutes. Mr. James is very clever to earn money and equally clever to spend it. He is using enormous sums in social improvement, educational enterprise not only in America but in Turkey and Armenia. He is stretching his hands all over the world."

For this first half of the cruise, *Aloha* had had enough wind to do a fair amount of sailing, although her company still felt that they had been short-changed on the passage to Hawaii. As it turned out, the good run from New York to Panama, the 290-mile day's run approaching Hawaii, and a few days on the leg to Japan, were the best sailing she enjoyed all the way around.

For the last 10,000 miles, she was continuously plagued by light air, or headwinds that were none too strong when there was any wind at all, and a square-rigged ship is not supposed to be much at going to windward. Down the China Coast, into the Philippines and on to Borneo, Java, Singapore, Penang, Rangoon and India, even in areas of reliably strong Trades, she met bafflingly light airs, and the coal was kept shoveling into her boilers to keep her on any kind of schedule. She actually only sailed for about 250 miles out of the 10,000, which is an interesting contrast to that 290 miles she made in one day while surging before the Northeast Trades on the way to Hawaii.

Despite the disappointment over sailing conditions, the guests continued to enjoy the exotic sights, scenes, sounds and smells of the ports they visited. In India they took the pilgrimage to see the Taj Mahal and were not disappointed, and after stops at Calcutta and Aden, the bark steamed westward over a hot and sultry Indian Ocean to the torrid Red Sea. This was territory many of them had seen before, though they still found Cairo fascinating, and a short stop at Beirut allowed them to see the ruins at Baalbek which many of them considered as impressive as any they had seen anywhere.

Commodore James did his own navigating

The Jameses visited with the staff at the American University in Beirut, and *Aloha* weighed anchor again the same afternoon for Marseilles. It was springtime in the Mediterranean, and as the ship moved into higher latitudes, her company noted the marked change in temperature from the long period they had spent in the tropics.

Threading her way through the Straits of Bonifacio between Sardinia and Corsica, she put into Marseilles on May 5, and for the owner's party the cruise had ended. They disembarked amid fond farewells and took off to sightsee the Continent and make their way homeward by steamship, while the professional crew took *Aloha* the rest of the way. She arrived back in Newport, R.I., on June 1 after a passage that had covered 28,827 miles in 259 days.

It had all been done with efficiency and ease. Fine seamanship had been exhibited throughout, and there were no horror tales or sea stories that anyone could tell about the passage. She had held mainly to the regular steamship routes and her passengers had lived in as much comfort, or more, and with even better service, than they would have if they had made the same cruise in an ocean liner. It was a circumnavigation as far removed from the hairy-chested exploits of such adventurers as Captains Joshua Slocum and John Voss as living in a pup tent is from a suite at the Waldorf, but in its way it was an epic feat of planning and execution that few other yacht owners had the experience, and the tenacity, to carry off.

Aloha settled back into the more conventional routine of yacht club cruises and East Coast socializing, content with the mileage she had covered, and was converted from steam to diesel. As thousands glimpsed her, as I did on that June evening on the Sound, they were lifted for a little while into a world that had gone, that of square-rigged sail, and into another that was going fast, that of the great private yachts capable of carrying guests in liner-like luxury to landfalls such as Penang, Hilo or Zamboanga.

Stately *Sea Cloud*

8

Sea Cloud

One of the great yachts defied the fate that befell her sisters, though for a while it appeared that she too would end up as a ruined hulk or a pile of scrap under the ship-breaker's hammer. Visitors in the early 60s to the troubled island of Hispaniola, which the Dominican Republic and Haiti uneasily share, were surprised, and, if they loved ships, shocked, to see a graceful square-rigger lying at a pier in the narrow Rio Ozama in the Dominican Republic.

Her beautiful white hull and tall spars seemed alien in the hot, tropic sunlight, against a backdrop of crumbling piers, Latin American slums and the muddy waters of the river. Neglected as she was, she had a clean, Nordic look about her, as though she belonged under the Midnight Sun, and that was where she came from. She had been built in Germany in 1931, but, after a varied career, had ended as the private yacht of the Dominican dictator, Generalissimo Rafael Trujillo.

When his notorious career ended under a hail of assassins' bullets in 1961, there wasn't much hope that the big four-masted bark would sail again, and she seemed doomed for the scrap yard.

While revolution and civil war raged around her, she sat there decaying by the day under the sultry tropical sun, and no one knew what to do about her. After the fighting stopped and a measure of security settled over the troubled country, someone was found to buy the ship, and in 1967 she showed up in Miami, completely refitted and refurbished, as lavishly as she ever had been in her heyday. She was put on a rarefied form of charter service at a ticket of $7,800 a day (not counting operating expenses), and the towering tracery of her rig became a feature on the skyline of Miami's waterfront, where legal problems have kept her largely immobilized.

This was an unexpected fillip to what might have been the finish of a long and varied history. How long her story will continue in an era in which she is as violent an anachronism as a Stanley Steamer at the Indianapolis Speedway can only be conjectured, but as long as she exists, she furnishes a dramatic example for the millions of 1970s pleasure-boat enthusiasts of what it was like in the departed days when being a yachtsman took millions of dollars for the few, instead of a few dollars for the millions.

Her newest ownership is hidden under an anonymous corporation and she is handled for charter by professional yacht brokers. Even her professional captain claims not to know the owners he is working for. Not many private individuals can afford the tab for her, but there is business among big corporations wanting to entertain executives and important customers, and in a few millionaires who want a taste of how their predecessors lived. Her crew consists of fifty young seaman trainees from Scandinavia, and she has been re-named *Antarna*, her fifth name.

The refitting and redecorating job supposedly cost well over $2,500,000, and it accomplished an authentic restoration of what she had been like in the good times. Most important of all, she has that supreme symbol of opulence afloat (Aristotle Onassis had to have it on his 325-foot converted frigate *Christina*)—gold plumbing fixtures in all the bathrooms.

Her paneling, furniture, draperies, decorations, cabinets, carpets and bathrooms all reflect a combination of modern materials and old-style opulence that has not been seen afloat in the United States since before World War II. By some miracle, her spars and sails were intact, though much of her rigging needed replacement. Any of the owners she had over her career could almost step aboard and feel at home, as though the clock has never moved forward.

Sea Cloud's rigging

The clock started in 1931 at the Krupp works in Germany, where she was built for Mrs. Marjorie Post Hutton, heiress to the cereal fortune and one of the world's wealthiest women. Named *Hussar*, the 316-foot vessel was to replace an earlier three-masted schooner of the same name and from the same designers, Cox and Stevens. The first *Hussar* was a mere 204 feet, though when she was launched in 1923 she was one of the early showpieces of a gaudy era. She provided a good idea of what the Huttons liked in a yacht, and what

Seaman Carl H. Peterson at the base of a mast aboard *Patria*

they expanded and elaborated on when they built the second *Hussar*.

The first boat's interior was unusually luxurious for a sailing yacht. Her cabins were referred to as "living room," "dining room," "bedroom," etc. when she was written up in *Yachting* on her commissioning in 1923. Her living room was of the late Georgian period in decor, with a Siena marble mantle over an electric fireplace, a chandelier, tiled portraits of naval heroes such as John Paul Jones and Admiral Farragut as backplates for her light brackets, and the furniture covered in hand-made needlework and English brocades. Her dining room was in French walnut, and the owners' bedroom was in the Louis XVI style with a base color of old French ivory and soft pastels to complement it. The bedside tables and desk were inlaid in sandalwood, rosewood and tulipwood. A two-page advertising spread was placed in *Yachting* by the Aeolian Piano Company to pay tribute to their product in her grand salon.

This sort of decor, and this kind of thinking was only the beginning for what went into the new *Hussar*. The 204-footer was by then overshadowed by the magnificent creations of the late 1920s and a new yacht that was just that much grander was planned. Before she could be finished, the dire doings of the Stock Market crash and its aftermath shook the luxury yachting fraternity about as thoroughly as any segment of the population was shaken in those dark days, but Mrs. Hutton was quoted as feeling that it was her public duty to spend money, both to bolster the economy and to spread confidence.

Certainly she helped the unemployment problem with a crew of seventy-two, and she also helped the clothing industry by ordering a complete change of uniform for everyone in the crew twice a year. The new vessel was 316 feet by 49 feet, drew 19, and her diesel-electric plant could drive her at 14 knots if there was no inclination to use her 35,000 square feet of sail. Her furniture and fittings were at the height of luxury, with such features as parquet floors, some Chippendale furniture, and marble bathrooms, and the touches of period elegance and special decor that had been such a feature of the first *Hussar* were even more lavish.

She was known as *Hussar* for only a short while, however. The

Huttons were divorced, and Marjorie kept the yacht. When she married Joseph E. Davies in 1935, the vessel came with her, and received the first name change—to *Sea Cloud*. Davies was appointed Franklin D. Roosevelt's Ambassador to Russia in 1936, and the Postum heiress and *Sea Cloud* were spectacular intrusions on the Communist ken. In 1938-39, Davies was Ambassador to Belgium and Luxembourg, and *Sea Cloud* was often used for diplomatic entertaining, a brilliant fixture in continental ports, but the gathering war clouds ended this phase of her career.

She did some wartime patrol service, and remained registered under the Davies name in *Lloyd's Register* until 1955, first as belonging to Joseph E. Davies, and then to Mrs. Marjorie Post Davies, foreshadowing their divorce in 1955, when Marjorie was sixty-eight and Davies seventy-nine. In that year also, the yacht was sold to Trujillo, reportedly for $500,000, though this has not been substantiated, and the dictator renamed her *Patria*.

Soon she had yet another name, when Trujillo, indulging his playboy son Ramfils, let junior have the family yacht in 1958. Like a homing pigeon, Ramfils headed for Southern California and such attractions of the Hollywood film colony as Zsa Zsa Gabor and Kim Novak, and he started calling the stately bark *Angelita* instead of *Patria*. Just as she had towered over European harbors when the Davies were entertaining aboard her in the 30s, she now became a spectacular addition to the Southern California seascape. Nothing like her had ever been seen on that coast, and even blasé Hollywood was impressed by the swinging parties Ramfils staged aboard *Angelita*. The sails weren't used much, but her lights blazed brightly late at night and music and the sound of revelry drifted from her anchorage across the dark waters.

One morning, harbor watchers had something extra to talk about when they spied lettering on the gleaming white sides of the yacht. During the wee hours, pranksters had painted large characters stating "Zsa Zsa Slept Here."

Eventually Papa's patience wore thin at the notoriety Ramfils and *Angelita* were getting, and he ordered the yacht back to home waters. He began using her himself, and had *Patria* placed on the transom

Sea Cloud in the spectator fleet at Marblehead Race Week

Sea Cloud stripped down after the war

again, and the yacht was to play a major role in the last days of the Trujillo dictatorship.

It was on board her that Trujillo reportedly twice made gloomy prophecies on his own fate. Once he turned to a group of his associates, at least one of whom was a member of the conspiracy that engineered his assassination, and said, "Which one of you will be the Judas who will betray me?" Later, sitting in the sumptuous surroundings of the dining room with two friends, he suddenly said, "I will leave you soon. I'm completely well, but I'm going to leave you. We will talk no more about it."

That was on May 6, and on May 30, the stocky sallow-faced man, who had ruled by terror and oppression, died by the violence of assassins' bullets.

Later in the year, when Ramfils realized that he would not be able to continue his father's regime, he took his father's coffin aboard *Patria* and fled southward down the Antilles to Martinique in the French West Indies, where he left the ship and took a plane to Paris. Still on board *Patria* was the dictator's body and an estimated $4,000,000 in currency secreted by the Trujillo family. Officials of the new regime were able to bribe the crew to bring *Patria* back to Santo Domingo, where the body was removed and flown to France.

After this last chore for the Trujillo regime, a far cry from the wild days and nights off Southern California, *Patria* sat there for five years, with a skeleton crew on board to keep her machinery in working condition and do basic maintenance. Two years before he died, Trujillo had spent $1,380,000 repowering her with four diesels that increased her speed to 17 knots, and she was still in basically good shape despite the effects of tropical humidity and blistering sun. Unharmed by the violence of civil war swirling around her, she sat forlorn and useless as several attempts to gain control of her failed, until her 1967 purchasers finally took her over for an estimated $725,000 paid to the Dominican government.

Few yachts have ever had a more varied career or lasted longer beyond their time than *Hussar-Sea Cloud-Patria-Angelita-Antarna*, and she entered the 1970s as one of the last symbols, an especially fascinating one, of an era as dead as the dictator who once owned her.

Sea Cloud after arrival at Miami from the Dominican Republic, with Trujillo's name still on transom before she was renamed *Antarna*

Atlantic was always a stirring sight under full sail

9

Atlantic

Although she was built in 1903 and what was left of her could still be glimpsed in a South Jersey harbor in the 1960s, the 185-foot schooner *Atlantic* gained undying fame as one of the greatest of all great yachts for one magnificent feat early in her career. She set a record as a pleasure vessel under sail for crossing the ocean for which she was named. That record is not likely ever to be beaten by a conventional single-hulled vessel. Her place in the record book seems completely secure.

Through the years after her record passage in 1905, she was a glamorous fixture of the yachting scene, and she never failed to provide a thrill for those who saw her long, lean, graceful hull sliding swiftly through the water. She won other races, and made another exciting story as part of the 1928 Transatlantic Race, but her place in history comes mainly from that one voyage. If she hadn't done it, she would be just another of the large, flashy yachts that symbolized a departed era.

As it was, she carried with her wherever she went the memory of her great feat, and it lent her an aura that other equally grandiose sailing yachts couldn't match.

Most of them were white, but *Atlantic* was a gleaming, raven black, and it seemed to add to the sense of power she imparted when she stormed across the waves under full canvas. Alfred Loomis, in his book *Ocean Racing*, said of her: "Whereas other schooners of her size seem to take to the water grudgingly, *Atlantic*, with her low freeboard and sweeping sheer, assumes the dignity of the sea and becomes one with the beauty of her native element. Her masts have exactly the right dissimilarity of rake and the silhouette of her canvas could not be more perfectly proportioned."

She was designed by William Gardner for Wilson Marshall and built of steel at Shooter's Island, N.Y., in the Arthur Kill off Staten Island. When she was built, there had been no Transatlantic Races since 1887, and actually the only ocean racing had been private affairs between rich men to settle wagers. Yachts of her size were used for short coastal races or afternoon events on Long Island Sound or off Newport, and the New York Yacht Club cruise was a highlight of each summer, with port-to-port day races.

There were stirrings, however, for an expansion of the sport, and a race across the Atlantic was discussed in 1903, with 1904 as the planned date. There were all sorts of international complications, as various prominent figures tried to get into the act, and interclub politics also played a role in the arrangement. Sir Thomas Lipton, the Kaiser, the New York Yacht Club, the Atlantic Yacht Club in Brooklyn, and various intermediaries were all discussing the proposed event, and it became so mixed up that the 1904 date was postponed.

The Kaiser, then at the height of his power and willful obstinacy, considered himself quite a yachtsman as skipper of the big schooner *Meteor* and operator of the opulent steam yacht *Hohenzollern*. He finally took over the proceedings, cut out all yacht clubs, and ran the whole thing through the naval attaché at the German Embassy.

The prize was to be an impressive gold cup, known as the Kaiser's Cup, of course, and there were to be no handicaps or sail restrictions. The only conditions of the race were that propellers were to be removed but could be carried on board, and steam power was not to be used in hoisting sails. The start was off Sandy Hook, and the finish was to be off The Lizard at the entrance to the English Channel, where a German warship would man the finish line.

As an indication of what yachting was like in that era, the boats were all manned by professionals, from captain to cabin boy, except for Robert E. Tod of Brooklyn, who was his own master and navigator on *Thistle*. One woman was in the race as a passenger in the smallest boat, the 108-foot schooner *Fleur de Lys*, a first in the sport.

Atlantic was put under the command of Capt. Charlie Barr, tough and wiry and the most successful racing skipper of the day, who had three times defended the America's Cup as a professional skipper —a thoroughly routine procedure at that time. Marshall and six friends went along strictly as passengers. They had no duties other than to keep their diaries and cheer the professionals along in their efforts.

They were only along for the ride, but what a ride! The start gave little omen of things to come, and in fact, the first date of May 16 brought zero visibility in fog, zero wind, and a postponement. The boats spent the night anchored back of Sandy Hook, and the morning of the seventeenth brought a little better visibility and a stir of air from the east. The eleven entrants, ranging from *Fleur de Lys* to the 245-foot full-rigged ship *Valhalla* owned by the Earl of Crawford, were towed to the starting area three-quarters of a mile east of Sandy Hook Lightship where a steamer flying an enormous burgee of the Imperial (German) Yacht Club waited to fire the noon starting gun.

The race had caused a great amount of public interest, with heavy newspaper coverage, and a fleet of excursion steamers and spectator yachts was on hand to watch the spectacle. It wasn't much, as the ponderous vessels tried to make headway in the light air, their sails hanging limply in the hazy light. Gradually they worked out to the southeastward away from the Long Island shore and disappeared into the mist to seaward. Finally the wind came in from the southwest, a more favorable quarter, and *Atlantic* squared away on the Great Circle course for the English Channel, a move that proved correct. The boats that stayed south or went farther north failed to find the best wind, but the big black schooner, with Barr crowding on every inch of her 18,500 square feet of canvas that she would take, began to make knots.

The contrast in the two types of lives on board seems stranger today than it did then, as it was in fact perfectly normal to have idle passengers on a racing yacht. While the professionals stood watch-and-watch in all weathers and conducted arduous sail changing drill under Barr's constant driving, the owner's party lived a life of pleasant ease in the main saloon and on the afterdeck. On the third day out, with the wind changing frequently, *Atlantic's* log recorded over thirty individual sail changes, but the guests merely sat by and watched, while being served sumptuous meals by white-jacketed stewards in the main dining room.

Not that they weren't interested in the race. They were like spectators at a football game, cheering and exhorting, and vitally involved, but their hands were only for writing log entries and clapping, not for heaving on rough rope and flailing canvas.

After a slow first day's run of 165 miles, the pace began to pick up, and the big schooner charged eastward, reeling off 222-, 229- and 271-mile noon-to-noon days before it fell light and she dropped to the slowest run, 112 miles. Then the wind, which had been mostly in the west and too far aft to provide a schooner's best point of sailing, backed more into the south, and even east of south, putting her on a reach, and she picked up to 243 miles, setting the stage for one of the great episodes in the history of sailing.

From noon of May 23 to noon of the twenty-fourth, 23 hours, 31 minutes and 30 seconds (changing longitude shortened the day), she charged through an increasingly rough sea at the incredible average of 14.2 knots. She was up in iceberg latitude and sighted some on the twenty-third, as hour after hour, with a great wake creaming away from her long lean after overhang and whitecaps charging up from the south to pass under the racing hull, she stormed along under full sail. Her awed passengers stood on deck in the cold northern air and watched the play of forces over the water and in the rigging, and Barr kept an anxious eye aloft. He was known as one of the toughest drivers afloat, and this was his kind of going. His only worry was that it might breeze on a bit more, forcing him to slow her down and reef her, but the breeze held steady, and the long, lean hull reeled off the knots for hour after hour.

When the noon sight was taken and the run figured, it came to 341 nautical miles, and jubilation spread through the ship, as a record of 328 miles that the schooner *Dauntless* had set in a match race in 1887 had been shattered. A double allowance of grog was sent forward to the hard-working crew, and the owner's party undoubtedly added to its own grog ration for the happy occasion.

These touches of passenger-crew relationships, bordering on the feudal, seem incredible to anyone who has ever done any modern ocean racing, but it was an accepted part of the life then. On one night, one of the passengers wrote of how beautiful it was on deck with the vessel making knots over a smooth sea, but the nip in the 42° air soon sent him back to the warmth of his sack, while the crew blew on cold hands and continued to work the ship.

Although the 341-mile day was the big one of the passage, and the major thrill for all hands, there was plenty of wild riding still to come as Barr drove the big vessel steadily eastward. The wind clocked around more to the southwest again and began to increase, and reluctantly Barr reduced sail, one by one, or sometimes had the wind do it for him before he could order a sail struck. By the afternoon of the twenty-sixth, she was plunging before a whole gale with only a squaresail and fore trysail still set, and it was a wild and frightening ride.

The question was whether to use caution and heave to, or to keep her driving despite the extreme conditions. Two men had to be lashed to the wheel to control the corkscrewing hull, and oil bags were rigged on the weather rail to cut down the sea's fury. Barr admitted later he had wondered whether she could stand the continued driving, but he made the decision to hold her to it, and the result was a run of 279 miles, amazing under the reduced spread of sail. Three more days of charging eastward through slightly diminishing wind and sea, as sail was crowded back on, brought runs of 243, 309 and 282 miles, and she passed Bishop's Rock, not far from the finish, in 11 days, 16 hours and 21 minutes.

Here the wind quit, however, killing the hope of a race finish in under 12 days, and it took her 12 hours to squeeze out the last 49 agonizing miles. Still she passed the finish at The Lizard in 12 days,

4 hours, 1 minute and 19 seconds, an average speed of 10.4 knots for the 3,014 miles, and her position in history was secure.

There was an ironic aftermath to *Atlantic's* great moment. It is not uncommon knowledge that the Kaiser failed to endear himself to the rest of the world in progressively more positive doses from 1905 on, and having won the Kaiser's Cup became less and less a sentimental coup through the years. The Kaiser became so obnoxious in his behavior, both political and social, that even his cousins among European royalty began to tire of his actions, and Edward VII finally had to put him in his place and call him for poor sportsmanship in an awkward confrontation. Edward admitted to tiring of Cowes Week, which he always had enjoyed, when the presence of "Cousin Willie" strained the atmosphere.

When World War I broke out, and anti-German feeling reached a peak of ill-will, Marshall decided to make capital on his possession of the Kaiser's Cup. While popular hysteria was turning sauerkraut into "Liberty Cabbage," he offered the cup for auction. The highest bidder's payment was to be turned into Liberty Bonds, and the cup itself was to be melted down, with its value as metal applied to the war effort.

There was probably greater benefit to the Allied cause in public relations in terms of suitably shocked emotions, when it was found out that the impressive trophy, when presented for smelting, turned out to be thinly plated with gold over base metal. It seemed to fit the popular conception of the Kaiser that prevailed in 1917.

Atlantic's next venture into the public eye came in 1928, the first time since 1905 that a Transatlantic race had been scheduled. This was to be from New York to Spain, and it was a curiously significant event, because it marked the changeover in ocean racing from the days of giant yachts, crewed by professionals, to the modern emphasis on smaller vessels handled completely by amateur crews, whose only interest in being on board is the chance to pit their stamina, muscles, courage and endurance against the combined challenge of other boats and the sea itself. The way this worked out is covered in the chapter on *Nina*.

The very makeup of the race dramatized this developing schism.

A division of large yachts, crewed by professionals in the old tradition, went off a week later than three smaller schooners with amateur crews, who left Sandy Hook early in July. Just before the start, the crew of professionals on the lovely big schooner *Elena* struck for higher wages and were replaced by lower-priced but green hands. *Atlantic*, now owned by Gerald Lambert, whose fortune came from Listerine, had a professional crew, but an amateur skipper, Charles Francis Adams, the Secretary of the Navy and the successful skipper of the America's Cup defender *Resolute* in 1920. Lambert was on board too, with other amateurs in the afterguard. This race marked the end of the day of the professional crew for ocean racing. Professionals lingered on in the America's Cup J-boats through the 1930s, but the 1928 race to Spain was the end of an era in offshore racing and the beginning of a newer, much more vital one.

Atlantic was naturally the favorite in the race, as no one could forget her fantastic performance in 1905, but this time, a month and a half later in the season, she didn't get the strength of wind she wanted in the North Atlantic, and her crew spent the whole passage grumbling about the lack of breeze. Early in the race she and *Elena* engaged in a boat-for-boat brush for two days at such close quarters that the crews could exchange friendly insults across the water. The wind was basically more to *Elena*'s liking as it was mainly from astern and she had a taller, larger rig, better suited to running, while *Atlantic*, as proved in 1905, loved to reach.

Atlantic's experienced and competitive afterguard had worked out a system for tacking downwind in an attempt to gain greater boat speed. Lambert had a special speedometer installed which recorded increases in speed when the angle of sailing was changed, and a set of tables was prepared to determine whether the extra distance sailed by tacking downwind was worth the increase in speed. This is a problem that has perplexed and fascinated sailors for many years, and *Atlantic*'s afterguard was one of the first groups to take a scientific approach to the problem. However, their system didn't seem to be reliable at speeds under 8 knots.

Although she had the same rig as in 1905, and some of the same crew, including the second mate, she only met her conditions for

144
Legendary
Yachts

the duration of one watch, when she stormed along at 17 knots, almost seeming to plane over the waves "like a hydroplane" as Lambert put it. Her runs were 167, 274, 245, 134, 173, 225, 137, 132, 196, 223, 235, 92, 81, 133, 290 and 202, far off the scorching pace she had set in the race to The Lizard. Once, when the slower schooner *Guinevere* hove into sight, Adams frantically adjusted *Atlantic's* sails until the other boat dropped from view, but it was not his race.

At Santander, jammed with yachtsmen, royalty, and just plain people attracted by the publicity given to the race, all expectations were that *Atlantic* would be the first boat in, and for several days there were false rumors that each time precipitated a mass exodus of boats from the harbor loaded with spectators, hoping to see the famous vessel arrive. One group of Spanish yachtsmen put out to sea in a tugboat and returned with the word that *Atlantic* was becalmed 30 miles offshore, and even showed packs of American cigarettes with U.S. revenue stamps on them which they claimed to have received as a present from skipper Adams. But these were all Spanish-type rumors.

Nina took the play away from the famous older vessel, and *Elena* actually beat her in, too, to win the King's Cup for larger yachts. *Nina's* eclipse of *Atlantic* turned out to be a valid, dramatic symbol of the changes that were taking place in the sport, and another incident in the race also seemed to dramatize these changes.

Near the end of the race, *Atlantic* came up on *Pinta*, one of the three smaller schooners that had been given a week's head start as their handicap. It was blowing fresh, and seas were running high, as the big black schooner ranged alongside the "little" 58-footer (which would be considered a big boat today). *Pinta* was reefed and plunging into a head sea, lurching and jumping and flinging spray across her decks, but, as they wiped the spray out of their eyes and peered from under their streaming sou'westers, her crew could see Lambert sitting aft on *Atlantic* in his deck chair, shaved, comfortably clothed and dry after a hot bath, and about to go below to a well-served meal in the main saloon.

Lambert said later that he couldn't help but wonder how human beings could exist under such punishment as he looked down from his comfortable perch at the wildly plunging *Pinta.*

Exist they have in modern ocean racing in far greater numbers than ever went to sea on the big professionally-manned machines, but the excitement and glamor generated by *Atlantic* and her sisters had much to do with inspiring the modern sport of amateur ocean racing.

This was her last major race. She took part in some shorter ones and New York Yacht Club cruises, but the Depression ended competition for vessels of *Atlantic's* size. Lambert kept her in commission, and whenever she swept down Long Island Sound or across Buzzards Bay under a full press of sail, those who saw her couldn't help but hark back to her days of glory in 1905. Whenever she got up to speed on a reach, it wasn't hard to imagine what she must have been like on that glorious day she reeled off 341 miles.

With World War II she went on anti-submarine patrol duty for a while, and afterward rode at anchor off City Island, N.Y., for a few years, rusting in disuse. Finally she was sold to the ship-breakers and was towed to the Delaware River to be scrapped. Her keel, the most valuable hunk of metal on her, was removed, but before the hammers went to work on her hull, a sentimental yachtsman named Ward Bright, who operated a large marina in Wildwood, N.J., and already owned a 12-Meter in which he day-sailed off the South Jersey coast, heard about *Atlantic's* imminent fate.

He had always admired her from afar and knew the story or her feats by heart, and before she could be dismantled further, he bought her from the ship-breakers and had her towed to Wildwood. Without her keel for ballast, she was a skittish thing, and she almost got in trouble rounding Cape May, but she finally made it safely to port, and Bright moored her to a bulkhead at his marina.

There were various plans for her. For a while he planned to fit her out as a floating restaurant, or perhaps a gift shop, but he was a sailor at heart and finally decided that this sort of thing would be too ignominious an end. He had hopes of re-commissioning her and taking her to the Caribbean, but a project like this was not an easy one, and meanwhile, she remained at the bulkhead, her great sticks,

Fleet at start of race to Spain: *Atlantic* at right

Atlantic at start of race to Spain in 1928

towering over the flat New Jersey sand dunes, visible for miles.

On a fall day in the late 1950s, a typical change-of-season north-easter, wet and wild, swept up from Hatteras and the Delaware Capes and proceeded to batter South Jersey. *Atlantic*, supposedly secure but unoccupied alongside her bulkhead, began to move restlessly, surging against the lines that had held for several years, while the wind direction was pushing her steadily away from the shore. As the tide rose with the storm, she began to surge more strongly, and suddenly a bowline snapped, letting the high sheer of her bow swing further out.

From then on, there was a chain reaction. Line after line snapped, and before anyone on shore knew it, the long-inactive hull was free. As though she had some sea-seeking helmsman at her empty wheel, with the wind right behind her and blowing directly down the Inter-coastal Waterway, the big black vessel headed for Cold Spring Inlet, entrance to the ocean for which she was named. Like some legendary Flying Dutchman, she made her own way for more than a mile down the Waterway, with Bright, now aware of the situation, in hot pursuit in the yard tug.

Just before she got to the inlet, she nudged in toward shore at a slight bend in the channel. The tug caught up, lines were put aboard, and she was brought docilely back to her berth.

That was her last fling. Eventually her plates rusted through and she sank. Her owner died in 1968, and at that time there was no answer to what would happen to her. Ironically, as she wasted away there, a sailboat finally exceeded her speed record for crossing an ocean. In December 1968, the French lone voyager Eric Tabarly, with two more in crew, sailed the weird and ungainly 65-foot alumi-num trimaran *Pen Duick IV* from the Canary Islands to Barbados at an average speed of 11 knots for the 2,600 mile passage. There were those that felt this strange-looking nautical Meccano set couldn't be put in the same category as *Atlantic*, and they were sure that no mono-hull would ever match her time. In addition, her greatest feat, the magnificent day's run of 341 miles, had not been approached by the trimaran. If only for that day alone, *Atlantic* is secure in her niche of greatness.

The 294-foot *Savarona II* was not big enough

10

Savarona

There has to be a biggest in every field, and, naturally, there has been one yacht that was bigger than all the other magnificent vessels ever built for the purpose of dazzling one's contemporaries.

Perhaps she may be outbuilt someday, but it is highly unlikely. Even if she is, Mrs. Emily Roebling Cadwaladar's 407-foot *Savarona III*, which cost $4,000,000 to build in Germany in 1930, stands as a special symbol. She was the biggest, the most luxurious and the most lavish, and she was, in effect, the last of her line, obsolete, a care and a burden even before she was commissioned. She truly marked the end of an era.

By the time she was ready to be delivered, the splashy optimism of the 1920s had been submerged in the gloom of the Depression. If she had been brought to the United States, it would have been impossible to pay the taxes on her, and she was only in commission two years as a private yacht.

She is of interest mainly because of her special role as acme and end of an era all in one, not because of anything unusual she did or that happened aboard her. A rundown of her specifications and appointments will give some idea of what the ultimate was in the luxury days.

Mrs. Cadwalader had had an impressive enough *Savarona II*, a

$2,000,000 294-footer delivered in 1928, with that recurring status symbol, gold fixtures in her black marble bathrooms, and she used to give her guests the sensation of being underway by turning on the gyro-stabilizer in harbor, which would set up a rolling motion in the anchored vessel. She was soon outbuilt, however, by several vessels over 300 feet, like Julius Forstmann's *Orion* and Morgan's newest *Corsair,* which destroyed her appeal for her owner, who made sure no one could outbuild her by ordering the mammoth *Savarona III.*

She was described at the time as being fully the equivalent of an express ocean liner, and there were many ships carrying passengers on premium routes that were no longer than her 407 feet, 10 inches. It is also safe to say that they couldn't touch her lavish interior.

The money that went into her came from the wire and cable business that produced that marvel of its age, the Brooklyn Bridge. The Roeblings were German, and they were engineers, and nothing but the best specifications would do. She was designed by the American naval architect W. F. Gibbs, an expert in steamship design as well as in large yachts, and built at the Blohm and Voss Yard in Hamburg.

She was 4,646 tons, 350 feet on the water line, had a 52-foot beam and drew 19 feet 2 inches. She had eleven watertight bulkheads, and three of them went right up to the top deck, so that she had three completely intergrated watertight compartments. Her six geared high pressure turbines could drive her at a top speed of close to 20 knots, and she had a fantastic cruising range. At 18 knots she could have crossed the Atlantic and back, and she could go 7,500 miles at 17 knots and 11,500 at 13.5. Unfortunately, she was also too big and too deep to go into many of the most popular yachting harbors.

Other engineering marvels included gyro-stabilizers to keep her from rolling, complete heating and ventilation systems, and of course the latest in radio direction finders, depth sounders and other electrical gear.

As for the owner's quarters, they were intended to put all Morgans, Astors, Vanderbilts and every other yacht owner permanently in the

Savarona III, largest yacht ever built

shade. There were twelve double staterooms, each with private bath or shower in a day when such amenities were not considered compulsory, and the decor was of course on a lavish scale. These rooms were in addition to the owner's own area, which was actually called the owner's "apartment," a new description for a ship.

Entertainment was to be on a grand scale, and there were a great many "public rooms," as they would be known on an ocean liner, to take care of any function that could be imagined. One wonders whether the owner and guests really wanted to see very much of each other, as it wouldn't be hard to get away from one's fellow passengers with a choice of smoking room, card room, sun room, lounge, veranda, living room and dining saloon. There were eighty-three in the crew.

All this came too late, however, and there was very little chance to enjoy any of it. She would have been lost to taxes if she ventured into a U.S. port, and before she was used very much, she was put out on charter and listed for sale. As the post-crash jitters deepened into the realities of the Depression, few could afford to charter her for $80,000 a month, not including operating expenses of approximately $20,000 a month.

A British yacht broker who had her listed wrote that it was the height of futility to expect any action on this sort of arrangement, and he was not at all optimistic that he could sell her at the price of $1,500,000, which was put on her not too long after she was commissioned.

There was no denying that in operation she was a fine vessel. She made two Atlantic crossings and proved that she could maintain her cruising speed of 18 knots through rough conditions while keeping her passengers comfortable. Her gyro-stabilizers, a new concept then, later applied to such ocean liners as the *Conte di Savoia*, seemed to work well, and set her apart from even the fanciest yachts that preceded her. The nearest she came to yachting in the grand manner was a circumnavigation of South America, actually an unusual feat for a yacht at that time, and she made an indelible impression in the ports she visited on the voyage.

She was a handsome vessel with graceful clipper bow, raking

masts, two raked stacks, and nicely proportioned deckhouses, considering her great bulk. However, she was a white elephant.

The despairing yacht brokers found no one to buy her, and the eventual solution to the problem was just as symbolic as *Atlantic's* loss to *Nina* in the 1928 race to Spain.

Just as it would no longer be possible to race sailing yachts with large crews of professionals, and the sport would depend on amateurs to keep it alive and eventually build it into a pursuit that would have amazed the deck chair sitters in the afterguards of old, so would big, lavish, private ocean liners go almost completely out of style after the 1929 crash. A few owners carried on bravely through the 1930s, less affected by the crash because of the permanent nature of their fortunes as opposed to Wall Street quickies, but they were exceptions, and so were the few individuals who managed the life after World War II.

Only governments and heads of states could afford to operate vessels like *Savarona* after the great changes wrought in the 1930s. Without benefit of yacht brokers, who would desperately like to have handled such a plum as *Savarona* as they braced for the dark days ahead, the magnificent white elephant was unloaded on the Turkish Government for $1,000,000 and given to the President, Mustafa Kemal Ataturk. Ataturk was a "benevolent dictator" who had formed the modern Turkish nation and ruled it as its appointed president from the early 1920s until he died. After his death in 1938 the government took over the vessel.

It is an interesting coincidence that both *Savarona* and *Sea Cloud* became the private yachts of dictators, albeit dictators who had quite different effects on their countries. The only yachts that managed to carry on in the traditions that were shaken badly by World War I and were ended almost completely by the Depression and the change in income tax laws that followed were those magnificent relics of an earlier age, the Class J sloops that competed for the America's Cup in the 1930s. It took some well-established fortunes to keep them going in those drab years.

Owner's stateroom

The grand saloon

Guest's stateroom

The dining saloon

The card room

Ranger at right racing *Yankee*

11

Ranger

They called her superboat. And she was—the super boat of a super era of sailboat racing. Nothing has ever touched the J-boats, the incredibly tall, graceful—and expensive—machines that raced for the America's Cup during the 1930s. It was the twilight of an era, but a grand and glorious one that left glowing traditions behind and a memory of big, swift sloops sweeping across the rollers of Rhode Island Sound that will stand in the mind's eye of all who saw them as long as there is anyone alive who can recall those Hitler-haunted Depression days.

No one will ever campaign a J-boat again, and they far outstripped all the machines that had preceded them, so *Ranger*, the super J-boat of them all, is secure in her niche in yachting history. Her career was brief, but it was brilliant. Perhaps someone would have come up with a design to beat her. Certainly lessons would have been learned in the J's, just as each supposedly "super" boat of the 12-Meter America's Cup campaigns has been outbuilt the next time. But the fact remains that in 1937 she was the last and best of her line, and her perfection and the deeds she performed were a great thrill for all sailors.

She was also the last of the Vanderbilt yachts in the grand tradition. Harold S. Vanderbilt achieved the pinnacle of his racing fame as her skipper, and no one in the family since has followed in his steps. He raced with distinction in smaller yachts after *Ranger* had completed her swift, devastating foray through the ranks of the J's, but she had to be the supreme achievement.

Interestingly, *Ranger* not only marked the end of an era, but also the bridge to a new one. Her design was a rare endeavor, a team effort between a veteran expert and a young newcomer. Starling Burgess, who had designed the two previous J-boat defenders of the America's Cup, *Enterprise* in 1930 and *Rainbow* in 1934, and whose father had designed nineteenth-century defenders, was called in again by Vanderbilt, who worked out an arrangement in which Burgess teamed up with Olin J. Stephens, at 29, a rising yacht designer who had gained great fame when his first brain child, *Dorade*, won the 1930 Transatlantic Race. Stephens had added to his stature when *Edlu* won the 1934 Bermuda Race and *Stormy Weather* the 1936 Transatlantic competition, and Vanderbilt wanted him in the America's Cup picture.

No official version of the collaboration has ever been issued, and both designers preferred to keep the ultimate choice of *Ranger's* lines a secret between them, but the passage of time has made this collaboration increasingly significant, as Stephens went on to become one of the great designers of all time and the reigning genius of the 12-Meter era that revived America's Cup competition in the late 1950s.

It was significant for still another reason in that *Ranger* was the first sailing yacht in history to be tested in a towing tank. It was an established practice to test steamships and naval vessels, but the techniques had never been applied to sailboats until Professor Kenneth Davidson of Stevens Institute of Technology in Hoboken, N.J. (named for the family of John Cox Stevens, first Commodore of the New York Yacht Club and moving spirit of *America's* campaign in England in 1851), pioneered the idea. Four sets of lines for the new boat were tested against each other by towing scale models in an old swimming pool at Stevens. The reason sailboats had never been tank-tested was that they had to be towed at angles of heel and while making leeway, factors which do not affect large powered ships.

At *Ranger*'s commissioning (from left): Olin Stephens, Rod Stephens, Harold S. Vanderbilt, Starling Burgess

Davidson worked out ways that models could be tested which included these factors. In this process, a towing carriage running on tracks over the water, with the model attached at various angles of heel and yaw, registers resistance and other important performance data, taking some of the guesswork out of the art of designing a fast sailboat hull. The models were also tested against models of such known performers as *Enterprise*, *Rainbow* and *Endeavour*, the British challenger in 1934. The latter had obviously been potentially faster than *Rainbow*, but Vanderbilt and his relief helmsman, Sherman Hoyt, had brought the American boat through in the closest series in Cup history.

After analyzing all the information from these tests, Burgess and Stephens chose one set of lines, and they became *Ranger*. Her overwhelming success did as much as any one factor in establishing tank testing as an important adjunct to yacht designing, and the science has become increasingly sophisticated over the years.

They had the lines they liked, and Vanderbilt had been asked by the New York Yacht Club to head a syndicate to build and operate the new boat, but getting her afloat and in commission was not such a simple matter in 1937. The country had just started to come out of the depths of its greatest depression when a dip back, a recession, caused new scares that year. The high-flying spenders of the 1920s had all but disappeared, and even the oldest, solidest families whose fortunes went back far beyond the hothouse growth of the 20s were feeling the pinch in many ways.

Vanderbilt could not find any colleagues to come into his syndicate, and finally he was forced to go it alone, the only individual owner of a Cup defender since 1887. He chose the name, as he had *Enterprise's*, from U.S. Naval history, one of John Paul Jones' commands.

Even the Vanderbilt fortune could not support a don't-spare-the-horses campaign, and every possible economy was effected, as the new vessel took shape. She was built of steel at Bath Iron Works in Maine, which was glad to get the contract at a reduced price to keep its workers employed, and her rig was largely scavenged from previous boats, going all the way back to some winches and other gear from *Reliance*, the 1903 defender. Reliable estimates placed *Ranger's* cost at about $150-200,000, and the total cost of her campaign at about $500,000, an interesting contrast to the $900,000 spent on one unsuccessful candidate's campaign in 1930, and an estimate of a million dolars for operating an immensely smaller 12-Meter in the campaigns of the 1950s (when it would have taken well over $2,500,000 to operate a J-boat by the most conservative of estimates).

The only new rig gimmicks on *Ranger* were a Duralumin mast and bar steel rigging. She used many sails from older boats, and even her designers reduced their fees. In 1937 it was good just to be working.

She was launched May 11 and set out amid a noisy serenade of whistles and cheers, towing to Newport astern of Vanderbilt's motor yacht *Vara*. It was a brave sight as the big white sloop swept out of the Kennebec into the Gulf of Maine, her tall new mast towering above the rocks and pines of the coastline, but she was an incredibly sorry spectacle the following morning when she ended up in Marblehead minus the fancy new stick, her rigging a cat's cradle of snarled metal on her deck. Somehow some of her upper rigging carried away early in the night as she rolled her way south over large swells, and the result was a progression of disaster. In a night of horror, her crew stood by helplessly while the rigging gradually worked itself loose, flexing more and more as the 165-foot spar began to whip around

She lost her mast on her delivery trip from the yard

in wilder and wilder arcs. It was an insoluble problem as long as she continued to roll, and finally, after a horrendous siege of banging and clanging, the big spar let go just above the lower spreaders.

With the wreckage removed, she was towed to Newport minus rigging and fitted with a temporary rig scraped up from spares of several of the older boats. It wasn't really right, but even with this makeshift while awaiting a duplication of her original rig from Bath, she made a shambles of the opposition in the preliminary trial series.

Her afterguard of Olin and Rod Stephens, Arthur Knapp, Zenas Bliss and Vanderbilt's wife Gertrude (first woman to sail on an American defender—as observer) spent an anxious time watching the temporary rig, ready at the first sign of trouble to drop out, as they knew it wasn't strong enough to take the strains the swift new boat could put on it. It held together, however, and her new rig arrived in time for the second set of trials.

So superior was she that she probably could have gotten by without the new rig. Her only rivals were *Yankee* and *Rainbow*, re-treads who quickly proved that they were completely outclassed by the new scientifically-designed super boat, and *Ranger* didn't lose a single trial race.

The challenger from England was T. O. M. Sopwith, a self-made aircraft manufacturer who no doubt would have been surprised had he foreseen that his name would become a household word in the 1960s through the comic strip "Peanuts" and the adventures of Snoopy in his Sopwith Camel fighting the Red Baron. With *Endeavour* in 1934, he had thrown the biggest scare in the history of the series into the New York Yacht Club, which had held the Cup since *America's* adventures in 1851. However, combined with the greater skill and experience of Vanderbilt and his afterguard, Sopwith had been hampered by having to use an all-amateur crew. In the J-boat era, only the afterguard was amateur. All the deck hands who did the physical work of setting, lowering and handling sails were professionals, often known as "Norwegian Steam" or "Swedish Steam" since most of them were Scandinavians. This was at least a step forward from the early twentieth century when the skippers too were pros, but Sopwith's paid hands had gone on strike just before leaving

Mrs. Vanderbilt acted as an observer during races.
Vanderbilt is just ahead of her at the wheel.

England in 1934, and he had been forced to sign on a bunch of enthusiastic but inexperienced amateurs.

Their hands weren't tough enough, and their muscles weren't toned enough to measure up to the rigors of handling the immense J-boat rigs, and they were slow in tacking and jibing *Endeavour*. These factors, combined with some bad tactical decisions by Sopwith, had allowed the slower *Rainbow* to retain the Cup.

Sopwith had the bug, however, and he figured if *Endeavour* had been better than *Rainbow*, the same designer, Charles Nicholson, could no doubt improve on her further. *Endeavour II* had indeed proved faster than her three-year-old sister, but Sopwith brought both of them to the U.S., along with his large, gleaming motor yacht *Philante*, one of the largest luxury yachts in commission in the 30s. He specified that *Endeavour I* might be substituted as the challenger if difficulties developed with *Endeavour II*, but he never really staged all-out trials between the two dark blue sisters. They spent all their time in busy-looking but meaningless tactical drills, while *Ranger* was giving them a taste of what to expect by swamping the trial opposition. It was soon obvious that no further trials were necessary, and on Vanderbilt's fifty-third birthday he was notified of *Ranger's* selection. No one could argue with it. *Ranger* had set a new course record, averaging 11.1 knots on a day of not particularly strong wind, and there was no touching her.

The Cup races were scheduled for July 31 that year to allow the J's to take part in more racing throughout the season. This was much earlier than the traditional September date. *Ranger* had won twelve races in a row when she was selected as the defender, and there was some muttering in her crew that the opening Cup race shouldn't be her thirteenth. This was solved by participation in two races in the Eastern Yacht Club cruise, and she won her thirteenth handily over *Yankee*, *Rainbow* and *Endeavour I*. The string ran out in the next race however, perhaps taking some of the pressure off, when Sherman Hoyt as guest skipper on *Endeavour I* brought her in first in a tricky wind and tide hunt in Vineyard Sound, and *Yankee* also beat *Ranger*. These cruise races from port to port were very different tactically from match races around buoys. There was, for those days, a large

Ranger's size can be detected by comparing it to the powerboats and the figures on deck

Laid up at Herreshoff's yard in Bristol, R.I., after the
1937 campaign. *Weetamoe* is at left.

Half model profile of *Ranger*

spectator fleet of 800 yachts and excursion boats out to watch the first Cup race in a light southerly breeze, and the Coast Guard had its troubles clearing the course. Those aboard the spectator vessels were not to see anything like a contest, and their memories of the day, and the rest of the series, have to be tied in with the spectacle of an era ending, not with any competitive excitement. The only element of suspense that ever entered into the races was when *Ranger* managed to foul the sheet on her big quadri-lateral jib while tacking once or twice, putting *Endeavour* temporarily ahead at the start of the second race, but *Ranger's* superior speed soon told. Her victory margins in the first two races were the largest, boat-for-boat, since 1887, more than 17 and 18 minutes. These were reduced a bit in the last two when *Ranger* suffered another winch jam, but it was still an extremely decisive victory, with *Ranger* setting a flock of course and leg records.

After the America's Cup series ended, the two British and three American J's set off on a pleasant round of fleet races on the New York Yacht Club cruise and for two special trophies, and *Ranger* won all but one of the races, again a fluky wind-hunt that *Yankee* lucked into. While Hitler thundered in Europe, the stately J's unknowingly played out a Twilight of the Gods of their own in the pleasant August days of that summer, and those who watched them will never forget it.

For Vanderbilt, it was, as he later admitted, the high point of his career, a remarkable summer of success, good feeling, lack of tension and fine cooperation with his afterguard. *Ranger* won her twelve match races by the astounding average of 8 minutes 10 seconds, and her twenty-two fleet victories by a seven minute thirty-seven second average. She sailed just five races over the regular America's Cup course and in three of them she broke five course records.

Although the two *Endeavours* remained afloat as cruising boats with cut down rigs through the 60s, the American boats were all gone by the start of World War II, broken up for scrap in the fight that ended Hitler but also spelled the end of their own era and the doom of the fastest sailing vessels, on all points of sailing, ever developed.

Part III

A CHANGE OF EMPHASIS

Aras in her postwar role as *Williamsburgh*

12

After World War II

World War II scattered the great yachts far and wide. Even if economic changes hadn't dictated it, the era was effectively ended by
what happened to many of them. The last *Corsair* survived to
become a cruise ship with a short-lived career before she stranded on
the rocks at Acapulco, Mexico, in 1948 on her maiden commercial
voyage. *Ranger* was broken up so that her metal could aid the war
effort, along with most of the remaining J-boats. Hugh Chisholm's
yacht *Aras* remained in government service as the presidential yacht
Williamsburgh, and those luxury yachts that had not been sunk in
war service ended as banana boats and cargo ships, or owned by
Greek shipping magnates or oil-rich sheiks.

Crews for luxury vessels could no longer be found, and even if
they were available, wages for a large crew would break all but a few
of the world's multi-millionaires. As an example of how times
changed, the roster of the New York Yacht Club included only five
power yachts over 100 feet by 1968, the largest of these the 118-foot
Vergemere, owned by Ogden Phipps. A few vessels, registered out
of the United States, such as Aristotle Onassis' 325-foot *Christina*
and Daniel Ludwig's 257-foot *Danginn*, still approach pre-war luxury
standards, and, actually, far outstripped them in efficiency and convenience. The emphasis however has changed completely.

Instead of a few dozen grand yachts run on the scale of an ocean-liner, famous enough to be household words, but a tiny field numerically when placed against the post-World War II surge in yachting, there are thousands of boats that bring a different kind of luxury to a much wider public. Stock builders sell hundreds of luxury cabin yachts in the $100,000-and-up category every year and beautifully appointed custom-built boats in the 70- to 90-foot range are a common sight.

These don't capture the public imagination, however, and no one follows their careers with interest except boat yard operators, waiting with mouths watering for one to come in and tie up for repairs, yacht brokers, who can make a year's salary on a single sale, and a small group of professionals who staff them and know their owners' traits and idiosyncracies. The boats with the glamorous names are the ocean racing sailboats and America's Cup contenders. Their feats are followed by the whole yachting world, and they have achieved a different kind of glamor that can be quite exciting.

What is it like on one of the more expensive yachts being turned out today? There are no longer stewards and deckhands to serve the owner and his guests, nor the firemen heaving coal in the stokehold, but it is still possible to indulge in one's fancy living afloat.

In space that would barely have done for the "grand saloon" of a *Corsair* or *Nourmahal* today's luxury yacht manages to include ingeniously arranged accommodations that provide all the amenities for an owner's party of about six. Not many yachts can handle a Broadway chorus line, or all the members of a Wall Street firm and their wives, but two or three couples can still wallow in luxury afloat.

Modern luxury is measured between 55 and 90 feet. The boat may even be (to the horror of the shades of the individualistic tycoons of the previous century!) a stock concoction from one of the large firms which turn out production-line models from 22 to 65 feet. The boat may possibly be charged off to a business firm, although Internal Revenue Service people made it increasingly difficult in the 1960s for yachting ventures to come under expense account living.

Instead of a crew numbered in the dozens, with soot-grimed stokers hidden below, the more presentable Scandinavian types

Largest private yacht of the era is *Christina,*
Aristotle Onassis's converted Canadian frigate

Some of the electronic gear that makes operation simpler on the modern cabin cruiser

Except for those of Greek shipping magnates, most other large yachts were government-operated. This is *Sotavento*, built in 1947 as the Mexican presidential yacht.

allowed topsides as deck hands and mates, captains with the dignity and personal presence of merchant marine masters, and a polished corps of chefs, stewards and maids to attend to the needs of the owner and his family and friends, today's luxury yacht is probably staffed by a crew of three, or four at most, and competent hands are harder and harder to find.

Captains are often glorified chauffeurs with little seagoing tradition in their background, and the rest of the crew can include one chef-steward, who also does the housekeeping chores inside the vessel, and either a deckhand or an engineer, depending on whether the captain is better at deck work or mechanical pursuits.

A good captain can command a respectable five-figure salary, well up in the junior executive class, and one who is reliable, sober, industrious, clean, brave and reverent can do very well on a permanent basis with an appreciative owner who knows how to treat him with the proper combination of respect, firmness, fraternity and generosity, not necessarily in that order.

The two big problems with captains are quaffing and cumshaw. One who does not have an alchohol problem is especially to be valued, and the general circumstances of life for a yacht captain make it very hard for him to avoid this pitfall. There are long periods of boredom and inactivity as the yacht sits in a marina awaiting her owner's whims. The atmosphere is usually one of relaxation and high-priced gaiety. When the owner is present, the drinking can often move into high gear. The professional skipper suffers a continuous assault of alcoholic temptations, usually when he is in a state of mixed emotions. He can't help but envy his rich employers and their way of life, and yet he usually must salvage his self-respect by simultaneously scorning the free and easy ways and the nautical helplessness of the owner's group. Some treat him like a pal in the best modern, democractic tradition and lure him into drinking bouts this way, while others, unused to an easy master-servant relationship in virtually servantless times, become overbearing and completely inconsiderate. Either approach is a tough one to handle, and liquor usually ends up as the key to both of them. It is a strong-willed and wise captain who can solve this problem, though of

Incredible, stock fiberglass 70-footer which served as America's Cup committee boat in 1970, is typical of modern trend

Opposite: Section of America's Cup spectator fleet, 1970, showing average size of boats and lack of yachts. Schooner is *Tabor Boy*, former pilot schooner owned by Tabor Academy.

course there are certainly exceptions in which the owner and friends drink moderately, enjoy life afloat, and consider the skipper a respected and competent professional.

The question of cumshaw is another knotty one. There are subtle ramifications and nuances, but the basic situation is that many professional captains consider it an inherent right of their job to receive a commission, tip, bonus, whatever term might be used to dignify under-the-table payments, to bring their vessel's business to yards and suppliers.

If they are not cut in on the bill they won't come back, and there is always some other place anxious for their business that will make some such arrangement. Yards and owners try to fight it in various ways, and a minority of captains refuse to become involved, but the practice has become an accepted part of the luxury yacht scene.

Despite the seamy aspects of the life, there is a hard core of professional captains who know their job, do it well, and are competent seamen, navigators, ship handlers and ship keepers. The good ones stay with one owner for years and, despite the strain it places on normal family life, manage to find some unusual compensations in extra time off at certain seasons, prolonged visits in areas of pleasant climate, and an escape from the routine of ordinary jobs.

The other jobs on today's luxury yachts are much more on a hit-or-miss basis. For deckhands and stewards, owners, usually working through their captains, are dependent on a migratory type population that drifts by the season to resort areas and picks up whatever work is available. Turnover in these jobs is pretty much continuous, and the alcohol problem is again a serious one on a bit more elemental level than the subtle temptations that can afflict a captain. There is little pride in this kind of work, no tradition to it or steady pool of available labor, and one solution has been to hire local people, especially in areas like the Bahamas, to work by the season.

None of this keeps a growing group of yachtsmen from using this type of boat. Where a dozen or two big steam palaces might have made up the whole fleet in the early days, over a dozen companies now turn out one or two luxury yachts a month, some even more, with prices starting at well over $100,000 for the smaller

Steve and Esther Newmark cruised from California to Maine
and back in 1968 on *Eventide,* a 53-foot offshore cruiser

ones. It is a startling sight to see them rolling along production lines in the builder's plants, and a glimpse at any big marina in southern Florida during the winter, Southern California the year round, and any of the premium yachting areas in season is an eye-opening experience.

A typical yacht has diesel power, probably twin, capable of cruising her at 12-14 knots, with a little extra for top speed, and would be loaded with every known electronic device, such as depth recorders, radiotelephones, radar, loran, automatic pilots, devices to detect bilge fumes, engine r.p.m. synchronizers, anti-electrolysis systems and many more. In addition, there are such amenities as hot water, TV, hi-fi and stereo systems, showers, air conditioning and heating, deep freezes, and the most modern galley equipment. All these are why one of the crew must have some engineering background to keep at least the majority of these features working at any given time, and why yard operators drool when such a vessel comes in to have work done.

The owner's party usually has a large saloon, comparable to an apartment living room, wide walk-around decks with several areas for sunning, a fantail (afterdeck) protected from bad weather by weather cloths or sliding windows and doors, for semi-outdoor relaxing, and three double cabins. The owner usually has the largest, but each will have its own lavatory, walk-in closets and all sorts of bureau space. None of these cabins need be especially large, but they will have all the comforts of home. The crew's quarters in the forward part of the boat might be fairly spartan, but the captain's stateroom will be almost as comfortable as one of the guest cabins.

Small boats for fishing, water skiing and utility use will be carried on the top deck, and there might even be a sailing dinghy or boardboat. A cruising range of perhaps 1,500-2,000 miles can be stretched if need be with extra tankage or on-deck fuel, and food for several weeks can be carried without difficulty.

Some owners use this cruising range. A California couple, Steve and Esther Newmark, cruised their 54-foot motor yacht *Eventide* from Los Angeles to Maine and back via Central America and the West Indies in 1968-69, but most modern luxury yachts lead a fairly tame existence, never straying too far from marina facilities. Many move north and south with the seasons, usually with just the professionals on board. Despite their luxurious appointments, they are still small vessels when it comes to going offshore, and few are used out of protected waters. They cruise in good weather from name resort to name resort where they are the focus of party-giving and short day trips.

While not in the tradition of drinking champagne from slippers, such yachts are inevitably the vehicles for clandestine arrangements, and many a vessel's passenger list would look a bit strange if checked against the *Social Register*, but there is nothing particularly new about this phenomenon.

A specialized adjunct of the luxury yacht field is the sport fisherman, very often the most expensive boat built, foot for foot. One name that stands out in this field, the Rybovich yard in Palm Beach, Fla., has had millionaires fighting for a place on its waiting list ever since World War II, and the handsome, fast, beautifully-built craft turned out there have been often imitated, but never quite equalled.

Most of this luxury remains virtually anonymous, however, at least to the general public, and the graceful, exciting queens of sailboat racing are the glamor yachts of today.

Each year, new boats come along to add to the annals of the events that make the sports legends—the Bermuda Race, the Transpac, the Southern Circuit, the Mackinacs, and many more, but many of them only hold the spotlight for a short while. Names like *Baruna*, *Bolero*, *Ondine*, *Windward Passage*, John Alden's *Malabars* are known in yachtsmen's homes, and their exploits could fill a book, and sometimes have, but the three whose careers follow in the next chapters have achieved an even greater measure of fame through the extraordinary nature of their exploits.

Exact's cleanly modern
appointments

Bridge and controls

Foredeck

Comfortable deck-house saloon

Exact is representative of
the largest-size yacht being
built in the 1960s and 1970s

Britannia, the handsome present-day British royal yacht

Jonathan III is a modern development of what used to be known as houseboat-type yachts

A Pacemaker motoryacht, compact luxury in a stock design of 64 feet

Rybovich sportfishermen, dollar-per-foot, represent the most
expensive pleasure boats now in use

Commodore Fales at *Nina*'s wheel after winning Bermuda Race

13

Nina

No boat has ever been more beloved than *Nina*. When she won the 1962 Bermuda Race at the age of thirty-four under her seventy-four-year-old skipper, DeCoursey Fales, it was one of the most popular results in the history of sailboat racing. When Fales stepped forward to receive the trophy in the big shed on Hamilton's waterfront where the ceremony was held that year, the full-throated roar that greeted him was probably heard 600 miles away on the mainland.

Aside from being well-sailed by a grand sportsman and competitor, *Nina* had so uniquely spanned the fantastic changes that had taken place in the sport since the 1920s and had been a familiar part of the scene for so many years (while her present day competitors were growing up from little boys to yacht owners themselves) that everyone in the roaring crowd felt almost a personal stake in her success.

In her first race in 1928, for which she was expressly built, she had beaten the great *Atlantic* in the Transatlantic Race to Spain. She had been classed as a little boat then, all 59 feet of her, and her largely amateur crew was racing against professionals on the big boats, the last time that pros dominated the crew list in an ocean race. By the time she won the Bermuda Race, she had become a classic "big boat" in comparison to the average ocean racer, and the first boat classed that way to win over "little boats" since 1950.

Nina's whole career is a dramatization of the changes that have taken place in the sport, and it is one reason she came to be held in such veneration by the modern sailors who competed against her. Like a nautical Marlene Dietrich, she evoked the wistful admiration of many long after what should have been her allotted time.

She went from being a little boat to a big boat, she started out considered as an ugly duckling and ended as a famous, romantic beauty, and, from being called a "rule beater" in 1928, she progressed to being upheld as an example of the fact that no rule changes could really make a difference to a sound, well-designed vessel. When she was built, she was a radical advance in the type of rig then popular—the schooner—and she eventually became an exception that proved the rule that schooners were dead as an ocean racing type.

She was built for the 1928 race to Spain, and her name was chosen because of her entry in it. Another entry was renamed *Pinta*, and for a while a *Santa Maria* was on the list, but she didn't make it. Paul Hammond and Elihu Root, Jr., two experienced sailors who were well known in business and social circles, commissioned W. Starling Burgess to design her, and she was built at the Reuben Bigelow yard in Monument Beach, Mass., on Buzzards Bay, hard by the western end of the Cape Cod Canal. Bigelow had never built anything bigger than a catboat before, and a few alterations reportedly had to be made in her sheer line when she was trundled out of the shop, as she was so near the roof that no one had really looked at her yet.

It was her maiden racing effort when she met the starting gun for the small boat division of the race to Spain off Sandy Hook, N.J., on June 30. The major race was supposedly for the big boats like *Atlantic* and *Elena*, and the little boats, three of them, were an afterthought, given a week's head start as a handicap advantage over the vessels twice their size. The big boats raced for the King's Cup, and the Queen of Spain had to chip in with a trophy of her own for the smaller entries when they were added to the list.

Nina—always a grand sight under sail

The finish of the race at Santander was one of the most exciting in the history of the sport mainly because of the circumstances surrounding it. In an era when royalty was still able to put a special stamp on anything in which it took an interest, the race stirred not only yachting circles but the publics of Spain, the United States and many of the countries of Western Europe as well, and Santander, a colorful yachting center in the north of Spain, was jammed with festive crowds awaiting the arrival of the vessels.

As anticipation grew, rumors flew through the excited crowds, and there were many false alarms. The King, an ardent yachtsman himself (but not quite good enough to beat the Queen when they raced against each other), was very anxious to greet the leading yacht as she arrived, and, on July 22, after *Atlantic* had been rumored as close offshore, a large schooner yacht flying the Stars and Stripes was reported approaching the finish under full sail. The King dashed to his royal launch and sped toward the newcomer, only to find that she was the cruising yacht *Shenandoah II*, inbound from Nice. Alfonso's opinion of this false alarm was heard by all within megaphone range as the ruffled monarch arrived back at the Club Maritimo.

Finally there was a sighting that was not a false alarm. A sail had been picked up from the lighthouse on Capo Mayor, and a huge armada of spectator vessels steamed from the harbor, fully expecting that they were to greet the great *Atlantic*. The King led the way in his own fast launch, followed by the American Ambassador in the pinnace of the cruiser *U.S.S. Detroit*, the Admiral in his gig, and almost everything that floated in Santander harbor, including a canoe, outboards, sailboats, fishing boats, rowboats and, unbelievably, a four-oared shell, all crowded to the gunwale. Even *Detroit's* band was jammed into her barge. As this motley fleet swept by the point at the harbor entrance, another false alarm seemed to have been given. The ocean looked empty, but just before a disgusted group decided to head back to port after still another frustration, a speck of white loomed on the horizon: it was a schooner. At first her hull appeared black, and murmurs about *Atlantic* spread through the armada.

As she neared, however, discrepancies began to crop up. She was heeling fairly far for such a large vessel, and it became apparent that her hull was blue, not black. Incredibly it was *Nina*, the smallest boat in the fleet. Excitement grew as she moved in and just then confirmation came from glimpses of her staysail rig and the number "2" on her sail. (She has carried it for her whole career.)

When she crossed the line to a loud bang from the cannon, there were whistles, rockets, yells, cheers and even *The Star-Spangled Banner* from *Detroit's* band, with the man on the bass drum valiantly trying to keep his instrument dry under the forward seat of the barge. The shoreline was jammed with great crowds, and the cheers that swelled from their throats fairly rocked the Capo Mayor lighthouse off its base. King Alfonso was so carried away with the excitement of the occasion that he leapt to the cabin top of his launch as it came alongside *Nina* and waved his cap over his head. Amid the din, he shouted "Well sailed, *Nina!* I congratulate you! I am the King of Spain."

Seldom has there been a more public and dramatic finish to an ocean race, where the usual scene involves slipping by some buoy on a quiet midnight, with no one but a sleepy race committee as reluctant spectators.

Nina had won the race on her ability to go to windward in the light easterlies that prevailed near the end of the race, which she ate up with her tall rig. Tradition-minded old salts had said that her lofty mainmast would never make an ocean crossing, but it proved its worth by holding up beautifully and allowing her to sail her gaff-rigged competitors hull down in the moderate windward work. She hadn't been too bad off the wind either, as she stayed close enough to catch *Pinta* a couple of hundred miles from Spain, when the downwind work quit. She sailed by to leeward as the crews exchanged greetings and conjectures on where the other boats were, and went on to finish more than a day ahead. The big boats, carrying on the tradition of a fading era in which professional crews did all the work while the afterguard sipped champagne and cheered effetely from the salon and cockpit, had had a pleasant ocean cruise, but the amateurs on *Nina* had shown the difference hard work and attention to sail drill of those in it for the challenge of the contest could make.

Many a boat has won one big race and faded rapidly from view, her win resulting from the flukes that can always affect ocean racing, but *Nina* quickly proved that she was no flash in the pan. She went from Spain to England and gave the new group of British offshore yachtsmen a jolt by walking away with their special classic, the Fastnet Race. This contest of just over 600 miles through the stormy waters of the English Channel and the Irish Sea is famous for the rugged condition encountered on the course, and in 1926 only two of fifteen starters had managed to hold together and finish. The local sailors were sure that *Nina's* light construction and tall rig doomed her to disaster, but she showed them up in convincing fashion.

In the early stages, running down the Solent from Cowes to the Channel, *Nina* was mired in the pack and there were sly smiles on British faces, but Sherman Hoyt, who had taken over as skipper when Hammond and Root had to return to the States, was unruffled. "Just wait," was his simple admonishment as he looked around at the competition. And as soon as the boats turned the east end of the Isle of Wight and headed down Channel into the teeth of the wind, *Nina* left the fleet hull down to leeward in a matter of minutes. For the rest of the race, she pressed on through a variety of conditions, with her lead never threatened except by the American schooner *Mohawk*, another veteran of the race to Spain. Off the wind, the gaff-rigged *Mohawk* put on a spectacular show, and she even shook the confidence of *Nina's* crew as they saw her roaring down on The Fastnet Rock turning point while they were on their way back after being first around the slender light perched on its jumble of rocks, with spray-flinging breakers hurling spume half way up the tower.

When *Mohawk* rounded and started back on the windward leg across the Irish Sea, she wasn't quite so spectacular anymore and ended up 60 miles to leeward of *Nina* on the Cornish Coast. *Nina* was doing so well that she came up on the British cutter *Viking* off Land's End, still on her way west. This meant that *Nina* had a 400-mile lead, and *Viking*, despite her handicap of 34 hours, prudently decided to drop out.

Nina had one more major win, the 1929 race from New London to Gibson Island, Md., near Baltimore on the Chesapeake, and then she was temporarily retired. Hammond became involved in the 1930

America's Cup campaign, and *Nina* sat on the ways, quietly deterio-rating and drying out, until an Englishman who had admired her feats in 1928 came to her rescue. This was Bobby Somerset, a leading British ocean racer whose colorful French pilot cutter conversion *Jolie Brise* had been beaten by *Nina* in the Fastnet. He came to Amer-ica for the 1932 Bermuda Race and, although he won no racing prizes, gained a permanent niche in yachting history by rescuing the crew of the burning schooner *Adriana* on the first night out with a masterly display of seamanship and boat handling. Ten of *Adriana's* crew jumped safely to *Jolie Brise's* solid deck, but the man at the helm waited too long keeping his boat in position as *Jolie Brise* ranged alongside, fell between the hulls when he finally jumped, and became the only fatality in the history of the race.

Before he sailed *Jolie Brise* back, Somerset saw *Nina* in her yard cradle, became one of the many to fall in love with her, and bought her in 1933 after selling *Jolie Brise* in England. Neither Hammond, who came along in the crew, Hoyt, who was also aboard, nor Somer-set realized how badly *Nina* had dried out and been weakened in her long sojourn in a cradle when they set out from New York for the Bahamas in February 1933, a risky time to sail in northern waters.

Under shortened sail before a howling northwester that coated her with ice, *Nina* logged 203 miles in her first 24 hours, but then, as she neared the Gulf Stream, she really began to leak. Before long, work-ing the pumps became a matter of actual survival, and a crew of as experienced a group of offshore yachtsmen as could be assembled at that time almost was lost at sea. Pumping constantly and working a desperate bucket brigade when the pumps occasionally became clogged, they finally made port by heading off for Bermuda, where Burgess was summoned to assess the difficulties and Bert Darrell's boatyard went to work strengthening the dried-out hull.

Nothing was basically wrong, but her long drying out period had loosened her knees and fastenings, and she had to be extensively beefed up. The real culprit causing the bad leak was a hole that had been bored in her bottom and plugged, but the plug had worked loose in the strenuous sailing, probably after the warm Gulf Stream had melted ice in her bilges.

Somerset eventually took *Nina* into the West Indies, but she was still leaking and many of her deck fittings began to pop out, and he finally decided not to take her to Europe. Instead she came back to the United States and was again put up for sale, sitting once more in semi-neglected state in a yard for two years before another "lover" came along.

This time the love affair was a violent, permanent one. Just in time to save her from some ignominious end as a bargain-priced hulk, New York banker DeCoursey Fales decided that the storied vessel still had a great potential. Never well-known as a yachtsman until that time, he bought her in 1935 and set to work rehabilitating her. There was no overnight sensation. Every season, working from a book Fales filled with careful notes as he sailed her, improvements were made in her fittings and rig. Fales came from horse country in New Jersey's Far Hills area and had only done a little cruising until that time, but each year his life became more and more devoted to *Nina*.

In his high-pitched nasal voice, he would talk for hours about the "old girl" to anyone who showed an interest in her. With a hand on his listener's forearm, he would launch into detailed discussions of her characteristics as an almost dream-like look would transfix his angular features, and this dedication began to show in *Nina*.

She glistened in spotless paint and glossy varnish, and her enormous complement of sails, including such special schooner items as gollywobblers, fishermen and all sizes of staysails began to burgeon with beautifully-cut new canvas. The rest of her career was probably fore-ordained when she won the New York Yacht Club's prestigious Astor Cup in 1939 and 1940, her first major wins since 1929, and she also became a boat to be reckoned with on the New York Yacht Club cruise runs. Just before World War II, she won for the first time an event that was to become her specialty, the 233-mile Stamford-Vineyard Race on Long Island Sound, and then she was laid up for the duration of the war.

She was not allowed to rot, however, and she came out after the war in better shape than ever for a three-year stint as flagship of the New York Yacht Club. Fales was forever after addressed as "Commo-

dore" by sailors everywhere, and despite the social burdens of being flagship, *Nina* earned new honors by taking first in over three-quarters of the New York Yacht Club squadron runs she entered, as well as the Cygnet Cup in 1949 going to the outstanding yacht on the cruise, while Fales was Commodore.

She also made an almost continuous habit of winning the Vineyard Race, and the Commodore kept putting the trophies that she retired back in competition for various phases of the race. It became almost a stock joke that *Nina* would proceed to win back her own trophies in almost continuous progression. No other yacht has ever dominated a single event the way *Nina* did this one for over twenty years.

She was so good and so consistent, while the schooner rig became increasingly incongruous as modern yawls and sloops took over the racing scene and other schooners gradually vanished, that she no longer was considered as a freak or an oddity. She became a more or less permanent fixture in the top racing events, always respected, always one of the boats to beat, and quite a trophy winner. Somehow her appearance seemed to improve with age. Fales's professional captain, Willie Carstens, took as much pride in her as the Commodore did, and every inch of her gleamed and glistened, even at the end of a hard, spray-flinging race. Her sail complement was continuously up-dated with new synthetic sails as Dacron took over from cotton, and the fantastic sails that could not be cut for any other vessel were all reproduced in the modern materials. Her rig and fittings were progressively modernized, but the same hollow mainmast that was built for her in 1928, and which was the object of dire predictions by the sailors of the gaff-rigged types of that era, has stayed with her through the years. Her original rig was called a "two-masted cutter," since there was a straight line down the stays from the top of her mainmast across her foremast and down to the bowsprit, and this was one of the secrets of her windward ability, but Fales changed it several times, raising the height of the foremast and shortening the bowsprit. This took away the "two-masted cutter" effect but helped her off the wind while not hurting her remarkable ability on the wind.

While she walked away with cup after cup in almost every event, her Bermuda Race career, starting in 1946, had only been marked by a third in Class A in 1948 and a first in that class in 1956 before she started the race in 1962. Many a crack vessel had tried this race time after time with no hardware of any sort to show for it, and *Nina's* reputation was already secure when she and 130 other starters hit the line in a moderate southwester off Brenton Reef Lightvessel, the last time the race was to start at a lightship instead of a Texas Tower on the same spot. She was the third oldest boat in the race and the Commodore was the oldest skipper.

It was not a particularly exciting race, especially when compared to the 1960 one, which had been hit by every variety of weather short of a full-fledged hurricane. The first two days saw idyllic sailing, reaching in a fresh southwester over moderate seas, with a full moon each night and shirt-sleeve temperatures on deck. The whole fleet reeled off phenomenal mileage, and *Nina* made day's runs of 200 and 214 miles. On Sunday evening, 30 hours after the start, there were several Class A boats in sight ahead of her, and Fales decided to reach off and keep her moving, rather than pinch up to stay on the direct rhumb line course.

By Monday evening, the whole fleet had caught up to the center of a big high pressure area that was sitting north of Bermuda, and the good sailing stopped. Most of the boats went dead for hours on end, but *Nina,* by driving off to the east, was on the edge of the windless center of the high and had only 12 hours of calm before she began to pick up zephyrs. With intense concentration, she was raced through the light stuff like a big dinghy. Constant sail drill worked her drifters, gollywobblers, spinnakers, genoas and other light sails, including one gollie called "the Monster" which was set on the foremast and clewed to the outer end of the main boom. She moved out of the calm area more quickly than anyone else, and was second to finish, close behind the big light displacement ketch *Stormvogel.*

She was a strong possibility as a winner from then on, and Royal Bermuda Yacht Club officials greeted her with pomp and circumstance when she arrived at Two Rock Passage, the entrance to Hamilton Harbour. She was ushered to the position of honor off the clubhouse, and there she stayed, as no one came along to oust her. As each finisher's time was posted on the big bulletin board above the

Her winning Bermuda Race crew, Fales third from right, back row

yacht club lawn and boat after boat failed to match *Nina's* corrected standing, a cheer would go up from the group assaulting the bar underneath the board. Everyone was naturally hoping that they themselves would do well, but for once in the history of the race the other contestants had a common sentimental favorite that they wanted to win as long as they could not. This was a unique phenomenon in the history of ocean racing, and the genuine feeling behind it was made very clear by the tremendous roar that greeted the Commodore at the prize award ceremony.

That wasn't the end of *Nina's* career, but it had to be the climax. She continued to win her share of shorter races around Long Island Sound, and everywhere she went she seemed to carry an aura of victory and pride with her. In the 1964 Bermuda Race she made a gallant attempt to repeat and was again second best to finish, but it was a small boat race on corrected time. In 1966, the seventy-eight-year-old Commodore, who had not exactly led a sheltered life and had been a vigorous celebrant of many of his victories, planned to race but found that he could not as starting time approached. Seriously ill, he was taken to the hospital early in June, but he made sure that *Nina's* crack crew, which had sailed with him virtually intact for many years, took her in the race. He died while she was halfway to Bermuda in the race.

Although the love story and the attention that only a lover could lavish on her had ended, *Nina's* career had not, as she was donated to the Kings Point Merchant Marine Academy, where young student officers could assimilate some of her matchless tradition as they trained aboard her.

As *Tioga,* her original name, first-to-finish, 1940 Nassau Race.
Note narrow-paneled cotton sails.

14

Ticonderoga

On a warm, dark night in July 1963, the press boat for the Honolulu Race tossed and rolled unevenly on the swells off Diamond Head.
Word had come in to the race communication center at Ala Wai Harbor that the leading boat in the race would be finishing sometime
after midnight, and the press boat had plowed out against the Trade
wind seas, spray flinging across her bow, to be ready for the big
moment. Flitting around her in the dark was a fleet of spectator craft
crammed with sightseers. Catamarans swooped by, their sails like
swift-moving ghosts, and running lights winked unevenly in red
and green as the boats plunged over the swells.

The puffy Trade wind clouds clumping over Diamond Head
glowed in the reflection of Honolulu's lights, and the whitecapped
waves loomed high, hissed, and fell away as they rode in out of
the night. The moist, windy blackness hummed with tension and
anticipation.

Then, just before the first anticipatory sense of excitement had a
chance to recede into the incipient boredom of a false alarm and a
long, rough vigil, a spot of light appeared far off on the eastern horizon. Very quickly, it loomed larger and confirmed itself as a sailing
vessel under spinnaker, moving in fast before the Trades.

In a short time, as we in the press boat moved toward her, we were alongside and swinging back to accompany her to the finish line, the engine of the press boat laboring at full throttle to keep pace. Here was one of the most magnificent sights in all the world of sailing, the big ketch *Ticonderoga* booming through the night at hull speed under full sail. Her lights were all on—running, spreader and masthead— and spotlights splashed on her two towering spinnakers, blue and yellow on the main and black and yellow on the mizzen. Standing high and full, they bulged into the night sky, pulling her over the big swells of Molokai Channel in a long loping motion, a great curl of wave under her distinctive clipper bow and a rush of foam along her side. She was some giant bird caught in the glare of TV spotlights and flashbulbs as the spectator fleet swooped around the fringes of the lighted area like moths at a lantern. The climax came when she surged through a brilliant beam of blue light stabbing out from the shore to mark the finish line at the Diamond Head buoy. The buoy's shadow swept across her main, a parachute flare shot up from her afterdeck in celebration, and whistles, sirens and wind-blown shouts filled the night.

In many waters and for many years, the L. Francis Herreshoff-designed 72-footer had been one of the classic spectacles in yachting, but seldom could she have been a more dramatic picture than she was that night.

Less spectacular visually, but more dramatic in the end result, was her finish two years later, when she pulled off the fantastic feat of breaking the "unbreakable" record for this 2,225-mile biennial race. It had been set ten years before by the ketch *Morning Star*, 16 feet bigger than *Ti*, with all that means in added sail power and higher potential hull speed. All the experts said that never again would circumstances coincide for a large boat to benefit from absolutely optimum wind and weather, and in any event there were no longer boats as big as *Morning Star* in racing trim. To break the old mark, *Ticonderoga* had to average an incredible 9 2/3 knots for the entire passage, little more than a knot under her theoretical hull speed, including some early days of light going. Spurred by a running duel with the 73-foot ketch *Stormvogel* and riding the edge of a tropical disturbance that had her surfing on big combers at close to 20 knots in

bursts, she once again swept through the electric blue of the light beam first, and her 9 days, 13 hours, 51 minutes, 2 seconds knocked more than an hour off *Morning Star's* mark.

Although she raced a few more times, making in 1966 the fastest Transatlantic passage under sail since *Atlantic*, the Transpac record was the supreme feat of the long and storied career of this graceful vessel. The racing ended in 1968, and, completely refitted with a luxury interior, she entered a new career as a professionally operated charter yacht.

Graceful she always was, and she did everything gracefully, except for her launching at Quincy, Mass., August 10, 1936. She was built as *Tioga* for Harry E. Noyes, and her launching ceremony at Quincy Adams Yacht Yard was one of the social events of the summer yachting season, with over 300 guests at the gala affair. "Tioga" is an Indian word for beautiful wife, and the graceful clipper-bowed hull seemed to fit her name perfectly as she sat in the launching shed waiting for the big moment.

Noyes' eleven-year-old daughter Helen smashed a bottle of champagne lustily as workmen pounded in wedges to raise the keel blocks, and the blow of the bottle seemed to give the boat a sudden shove, though it was only a coincidence. The delighted cheers of the gathering at the efficient shattering of the bottle changed in mid-throat to high pitched screams as the cradle started to collapse on the starboard side just as the bowsprit slid out from under the shed. *Tioga* lurched, then careened back to port as she sped on down on her own, leaving the cradle behind. Her sailing master John Ryn, togged out in brand new uniform for the ceremony, was thrown off the bow on the lurching ride but was picked up unharmed, if damp, from the water, and *Tioga's* mad dash to meet her natural element was stopped by an attending powerboat before she got to the other shore.

Rather than a bad omen, her launching was taken by local salts as a sign that she could handle herself in a tough spot.

She was not intended as an ocean racer, but as an overgrown daysailer and cruising yacht for the Noyes family. She had all the amenities of that era for cruising comfort, including electric refrigeration and deep freeze, central heating, hot and cold running water, two

Under full sail on her way to first-to-finish Jamaica Race

ship-to-shore telephones and oversize fuel and water tanks. Most of these were unusually deluxe for a sailing yacht of the 1930s, and they also meant a great deal of extra weight if she ever did go into a race.

Herreshoff did not design her to fit any measurement rule, but to be a basically fast and seaworthy hull along the lines of Salem pilot boats. Two previous smaller boats from Herreshoff's board followed this inspiration, the second one being the first *Tioga*, a 58-footer Harry Noyes bought second hand, and he liked her so much that he commissioned Herreshoff to design a larger boat along the same lines. She showed a strong resemblance to such traditional influences as *America*, *Sappho* and *Magic* with her clipper bow, long, straight keel and beautiful run aft.

It can hardly be said that she burst upon the racing scene as a herald of a new age of speed. In her debut in the Jeffrey's Ledge Race in September 1936, in what really amounted to a tune-up for her, she was third from last after some troubles with rigging and crew seasickness. In her first two races on the Southern Circuit that winter, she also failed to set the world on fire but she did engage down there in some of the pleasant cruising for which she was intended.

It wasn't until she got back north that she won her first race, Boston Corinthian's Grand Handicap Chowder race, a 15-miler in a heavy blow. The big ketch charged through the chop to finish 34 minutes ahead of the second boat and save her time. One 15-mile chowder race is not anything much to build a reputation on, but the following spring she made the first of her record runs offshore.

This was in a 171-mile race from New London to Marblehead around the outside of Cape Cod in a southwester that soon built to over 30 knots. She boomed through Vineyard and Nantucket Sounds and up the back of the Cape at well over 10 knots and then close-reached across Massachusetts Bay to finish in 18 hours, 37 minutes at an average of 9.2 knots, held down by light going at the start. For most of the course she had averaged close to 11, and she broke the course record, set by Morgan Plant's majestic 136-foot schooner *Elena* in 1911, by almost 2 hours. By now the yachting world knew that, when given the proper conditions, the big powerful ketch with the fine lines of a clipper could really step out.

It wasn't until 1940 that she broke another course record, and this one stood for twenty-six years. The three-legged Miami-Nassau Race usually combines several points of sailing, but that year the wind started in the southeast and gradually swung to southwest, making a reach all the way, just the conditions for *Tioga's* long-waterlined hull, and she ate up the miles. It breezed on to 30-35 knots on a clear, moonless night, and sails began to blow throughout the fleet, while one mast went over the side. *Tioga* popped a jib sheet but preventers held and saved the sail, and she swept down Northwest Providence Channel with an escort of whitecaps flashing in the early morning sun to finish in 19:36:30, taking 43 minutes off the record set by the 72-foot ketch *Vamarie*. Despite her 9.4-knot performance, she lost the corrected finish by three minutes to the yawl *Stormy Weather*, which had made a private thing out of winning this race. It wasn't until 1966 that the 72-foot yawl *Escapade* shaved three minutes off the mark for the 184-mile course in a race sailed in a fresh norther that swung northeast. Ironically, in 1965, *Ticonderoga* had failed by less than a minute to break her own record, set as *Tioga*, in a race that was very similar to the 1966 one in conditions.

The Miami-Nassau record was her last major feat as *Tioga*. Noyes was killed in an airplane crash in 1941 and the boat was laid up until the Coast Guard took her over for offshore patrol work. In July 1942, she was painted gray, armed with a small machine gun and sent out of Boston on anti-submarine picket duty as CGR2509. The theory of this patrol was that silent sailboats could hold station while submarines would be unable to pick up machinery noises on sound detection gear. The sailboats could then report any subs that came to the surface without realizing anyone was there.

She had no spectacular encounters with the enemy and her toughest encounter of the war was with a drawbridge on a trip to Norfolk, Va. In a mix-up, the operator lowered the bridge on her mainmast, breaking it off in the middle. Repairs were made with glue and screws by the Navy without unstepping the mast, a procedure that was to return and haunt her later.

In 1946 she received a new owner, a new name and a new coat of white paint. Allan P. Carlisle bought her and renamed her *Ticon-*

deroga (inserting the letters "conder" between those of her original name) which remained with the Noyes family and has been used by them since for many more yachts. Adorned with this fine old American name, she went on to new and greater glory, but not right away,

Her first race was the 1947 Miami-Nassau event, under charter to Dr. Matthew T. Mellon, and she was forging out a good lead over the fleet in the teeth of a strong easterly and rough sea when the wartime repairs to the mast let go and the mainmast collapsed, taking the mizzen with it.

Back north, with a new stick, she set another course record by sweeping over the Marblehead-Halifax course of 366 miles in 50:16: 25 enveloped in pea soup fog all the way, and this time she was far enough ahead of the next boat, 10½ hours over Rod Stephens' *Mustang*, to save her time and take corrected first.

For the next few years, Carlisle chartered *Ticonderoga* out for many of the southern races, and she was always a contender for first-to-finish if she had her conditions, but record-book performances eluded her, and in 1951 she was sold to John Hertz, Jr., of New York. Hertz, of the car rental family, had *Ti*, as she was increasingly coming to be called, completely overhauled and refitted and he took her south for the 1952 Southern Ocean Racing Conference (S.O.R.C.). She set a course record of 3:37:41 in the 30-mile Nassau Cup Race, but it was in the nineteenth annual St. Petersburg-Havana Race in March that she achieved another one of her moments of lasting glory with a performance for the record book. This may be one that stays permanently in the record-book, as in 1960 the race fell a victim of the Castro upheaval.

The 284-mile St. Petersburg-Havana Race was the original one of the Southern Circuit and did much to glamorize this winter ocean racing. It was a good race course through the three very different bodies of water—Tampa Bay, the Gulf of Mexico and the Straits of Florida, with its rushing Gulf Stream. At the finish, the bright lights of Havana were a lure for sea-weary sailors, and many a wife used to wonder why her husband was never very insistent that she follow the fleet to the Cuban capital. Hospitality at all levels, from white-flanneled formality to legendary bordello high jinks, awaited the competitors, and word spread throughout the yachting world that this was the one to go on, even if you could only get away for one race.

Political upheavals made life just as interesting as the more gentle delights, and 1952 was one of those years. There is one story of a boat crossing the finish line off Morro Castle just as a burst of gunfire swept over the harbor, putting a neat row of holes across the middle of the boat's mainsail. The man at the wheel looked up, saw the holes, and is supposed to have said, "Well, I guess we can put in another row of reef points now."

Batista was just coming to power with a coup that kept him there until Castro deposed him on New Year's Day 1959, but until the Communists made life vastly different on "The Pearl of the Antilles," a little thing like a political coup never bothered anybody unless he happened to meet one of the bullets. Fortunately none of the yachtsmen did.

Perhaps it was the distraction of gunfire on shore, or perhaps just the surprise of *Ticonderoga's* early arrival, but the race committee forgot the finishing cannon. They hadn't even manned the line yet when *Ti's* sails appeared over the lumpy horizon of a wind-blown Gulf Stream, so they jumped in a power boat sans cannon and compromised by all shouting "Hooray" as a finishing signal when *Ti's* graceful clipper bow swept by.

It was a suitable salute to a fine performance, as she had covered the distance in 31:36:15 at better than 9 knots, knocking 3½ hours off the old mark. The wind had been moderate from the northeast for an easy slide down the Gulf, but it had veered more into the east and howled up to more than 40 in the puffs, kicking up a heavy sea against the Stream. The Coast Guard cutter clocking these wind velocities reported watching *Ti* surf by at close to 13 knots on the point of sailing she liked best—a reach. While others suffered blown sails, lost stays and dismastings, she held together well for what was the finest performance, till then, of her career.

This gave her the course record for all the S.O.R.C. races, a distinction she alone has held, and she later added to it in 1962 by setting the mark in the Havana Race's replacement, the St. Pete—Fort Lauderdale Race.

Racing off Nassau

Being rebuilt for charter service

A party spread for charter guests

Hertz took her abroad and cruised and raced her for 12,000 miles, and it was on the return passage that she set a remarkable record of one 264-mile day's run and a three-day noon-to-noon run of 667 miles before the northeast Trades between St. Thomas and Miami, a burst of speed rivalling the record runs made by 300-foot clipper ships under a full press of square-rigged canvas.

One race that eluded *Ti* was the Bermuda Race, which is not suited to her special qualities. On this 635-mile thrash from cold New England water across the Gulf Stream to the warm blue seas of Bermuda, there is usually a good amount of windward work, and a variety of wind conditions, with very little chance for the long reaching or running passages that allow *Ti* to show herself at her best. She tried it several times without notable success, and had the same experience in light and variable going on the Great Lakes.

After five years, Hertz sold her to Baxter Still of Miami, who operated her mostly for charter. Still sold her in 1959 to William Brittain of Ann Arbor, Mich., who was so impressed by her reputation that he bought her sight unseen. She was chartered out quite often for racing and cruising, and it wasn't until she hit the Honolulu trail that she found another glory road to the record book. She tried this 2,225-mile downwind classic, made to order for her if it blows hard enough, in 1961 and finished second to the big M-boat *Sirius*, after an exciting boat-for-boat duel.

Then, in 1963, she found the right man to make the most of her qualities in the Transpac. *Ti* has, like *Nina*, always been a boat that people fall in love with in a special way, and Robert Johnson of Portland, Ore., ended up having a very special love affair with the twenty-seven-year-old queen.

Johnson, whose family developed one of the biggest plywood businesses in the country, had cut a wide swathe in various yachting circles as a man who could put on quite a party, even in the middle of a race. A heavy-set man in his forties, he hadn't been considered a serious racing skipper before, but for the Transpac that year, he asked some experienced West Coast sailors to assemble a top-notch racing crew and really give the old lady a ride to Diamond Head. Just such a crew was signed on and was eager to go, when a sudden contretemps developed as starting day, July 4, approached. Her professional captain, who had sailed the boat around from the East Coast with a skeleton crew, informed Johnson that he and his crew would operate the boat, and that there was room for a few of his friends as long as they understood who was really racing the boat.

Since Johnson had a complete crew ready to go, the area of misunderstanding was rather large, and in fact became so vast that a court order was eventually needed to settle the situation. Given legal clearance a mere few hours before the noon start, the crew that Johnson and friends had put together hardly had a speaking acquaintance with *Ti* when they were towed out to the starting line, as they had decided that she would do better with her propeller removed.

While thousands of spectator boats buzzed around them after the light wind start, they took sail inventory and became familiar with her workings, and soon they had her moving well offshore. She took Johnson's fancy so well, in fact, that he reportedly radioed Brittain in mid-race saying "I'll buy her as is, where is, for $50,000."

The deal wasn't that easily consummated, but he did end up buying her, not necessarily for that sum, and set out on an intensive two-ocean campaign dedicating himself completely to the program. The grand old vessel had begun to show her age, and she was extensively rebuilt, with a stripped-down interior laid out for racing to replace her traditional cruising arrangements that had had the same layout since she was built. Johnson had become a serious, dedicated ocean racing man, who seemed to think only of his boat.

In 1964 she set out to conquer a new world, the Tahiti Race, and she managed to break the course record, held by the same *Morning Star* whose Transpac record she was to break a year later. She made the 3,600 mile course in 17 days 6 hours, mostly on a spinnaker run on which chafe of halyards and sails became a real problem. To average almost 9 knots for such a distance was another fantastic feat, and she had one sprint of an hour in which she logged 16. She arrived in the middle of the riotous Bastille Day festivities, and reportedly she and her crew enhanced them considerably, before setting off on a history-making, at least in its local impact, cruise back though Les Iles sous le Vent, the "Out Islands" off Tahiti.

Deck view, in cruising trim

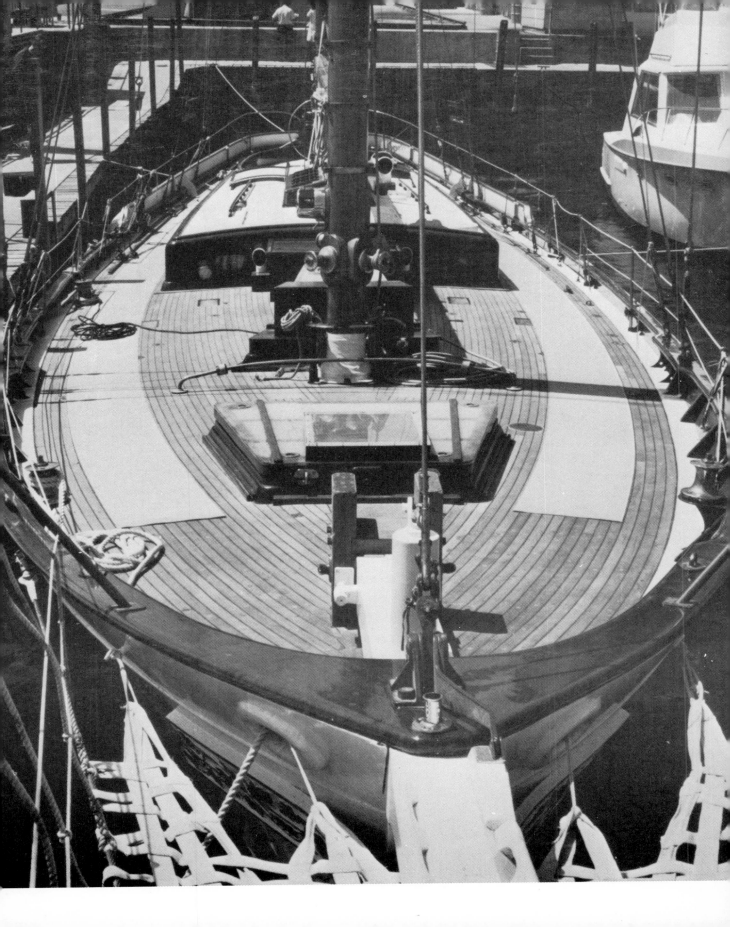

In 1965 she hit what was to be the peak of her long racing career. On the S.O.R.C. her West Coast crew had her cranked up for the usual spate of first-to-finish honors, and there was an ironic twist to the finish of the Miami-Nassau Race. Pushed by a fresh norther that had caused fantastic gyrations in some of the fancy new short-keeled boats in the fleet, *Ti* had stormed across the Gulf Stream steady as a church and was charging down on Nassau early in the morning hell-bent to break her 1940 record. With her crew straining to get every inch out of her, she suddenly ran afoul of the cruise ship *Bahama Star*. As a measure of *Ti's* speed, the liner had left Miami three hours after the race start and had taken all this time to catch the flying ketch. Unfortunately, she caught her right at the finish off Hog Island light at the entrance to Nassau, and, moving in for a number of minutes so her passengers could get a good look, came close aboard to windward and took *Ti's* wind. At the finish, *Ti* was just 32 seconds short of her 1940 time, and if looks were torpedos, *Bahama Star* would have been a shattered wreck.

Still another course record fell to her as she headed back to the West Coast via the Miami-Montego Bay Race to Jamaica and brought her own wind in behind her in a passage of 4:23:08:57 that left everybody else becalmed astern of her, giving a sweep of elapsed and corrected honors.

Then came her supreme performance, incredibly thrilling, shattering the record in the 1965 Transpac. Aside from the drama of doing the impossible and breaking *Morning Star's* mark, there was the fantastic boat-for-boat duel with *Stormvogel*. After roller-coasting along the edge of a tropical depression, sometimes surfing at such a pace that her speed indicator went off the top of the dial at 20 knots while her crew screamed like banshees and sails blew out of their bolt ropes, *Ti* saw *Stormvogel* burst suddenly out of a rain squall and cross tracks with *Ti* only a few hundred feet ahead. From there, the two raced the final 75 miles down Molokai Channel like a couple of Olympic yachts on a closed course, only it was blowing 40 knots on a pitch black night, as 30-foot seas reared under them. *Stormvogel* tacked down wind on a zig-zag course, going for maximum speed over more distance, while *Ti* rode the rhumb line, staying with it by executing a dip-pole jibe under jury-rigged spinnaker gear. Her 3,800-sq.-ft. spinnaker never collapsed for an instant during the tricky maneuver. (It would have been ripped to shreds if it had.) Bob Dickson at the helm kept her long-keeled, sea-kindly hull in the groove, she stayed between *Stormvogel* and the finish, and when she swept by the Diamond Head buoy, missing it by a few feet, she had a 5-minute-48-second lead and the incredible record. Perhaps Francis Herreshoff had never pictured this hull surfing over steep Pacific rollers when he put it on a drawing board in 1936, but the boat and the conditions had come together to write sailing history as though they had been fore-ordained. It could never have been written as fiction.

Finisterre

15

Finisterre

The 1960 Bermuda Race was the slowest in the history of this 635-mile ocean racing classic, run every even-numbered year from Newport, R.I., across the Gulf Stream to the Onion Patch. Beset by fog and calms in its early stages, it erupted into the heaviest dose of weather ever to hit the race. The 135-boat fleet struggled through squally winds that gusted to hurricane strength in the top puffs, and there were knockdowns, a man overboard (miraculously recovered), dis-mastings and disablings.

Blinking in the bright sunshine of perfect Bermuda weather when they finally made it there, the sea-weary sailors found it very hard to believe that, for the third race in a row, the same boat had won, surviving all the extra perils of this trouble-laden race. Never before had one boat taken the top prize three times, even when the fleet was much smaller in the 20s and 30s, and the percentages were better for pulling off a "hat trick" like this.

The cause of all this consternation and admiration, albeit somewhat grudging from some of her more consistently humiliated competitors, was a squat, beamy 38-foot yawl named *Finisterre*. When her light gray hull rode proudly in the honor mooring spot off the Royal Bermuda Yacht Club, she was just about the smallest boat in the racing fleet that jammed the harbor in colorful array.

As a "great yacht," she would seem an unlikely candidate against the stately J-boats, the *America*, *Sea Cloud* and *Aloha*, and she practically could have been carried in davits on *Savarona III*, but great she was in performance and influence, and she ranks as one of the most significant yachts in the history of the sport.

Although tiny against the standards of a departed day, she represented a type of development in racing effectiveness, in comfort aboard in relation to size, and in the quality of her design, workmanship, gear, fittings and appointments that bespoke top-notch quality in every way. Dollar-per-foot she probably represented as high a price as any of the luxury giants, and she carried this air of quality with a jaunty assurance and confidence that made her truly distinctive.

Naturally she became the most imitated, "improved" and "developed" design in the history of ocean racing. Carbon copies, near-replicas and later models came out by the hundreds, but none of them ever matched her in accomplishment or special aura. There has only been one *Finisterre* in the history of ocean racing.

She was the brainchild of a meticulous man with the time, money, self-confidence and imagination to get exactly what he wanted. Carleton Mitchell was a well-known yachtsman who had won his share of ocean-racing prizes and carried out some very successful and interesting cruises in boats that he had bought second hand. When the time came for him to have a boat custom-designed and built, he knew exactly what he wanted, and he got it. He even wrote some articles in *Yachting* magazine saying exactly what he was doing and why. He had figured out what it took to win prizes in ocean racing, especially the prestigious Bermuda Race, and he wanted this combined with a boat that would be comfortable, in fact luxurious, for cruising, and easy to handle.

For a designer, he went to the firm of Sparkman and Stephens, and he worked closely with Olin Stephens in seeing that his ideas were translated into a finished design.

Mitchell had started sailing as a boy in New Orleans, knocked about the islands some as a sailor and photographer, and acquired both sailing experience and a taste for topnotch quality. He first became known beyond his own circle of friends when he cruised his 46-foot ketch *Carib*, formerly John Alden's *Malabar XII*, from Trinidad to Florida via the Lesser Antilles and Bahamas right after World War II. The book he wrote about the cruise, *Islands to Windward*, remains a classic of the area, and of cruising literature, and has stirred many a dream.

Mitch wanted to race too, and *Carib* was outmoded for that. He moved up to *Caribbee*, a Rhodes-designed 58-foot centerboarder. In her he had some racing success and did a lot of cruising in the Bahamas and in Northern Europe, and he developed a respect for the sailing qualities of a beamy centerboarder. *Caribbee* had been built in 1937, and the type was generally out of favor in the early 50s, an era of deep-keeled, long-ended ocean racers of fairly narrow beam, but her ability to slog to windward in a sea, her roominess and comfort below, and her seakeeping qualities pleased him greatly.

However, she was a bit bigger than he wanted for cruising with a manageable group, she needed a big crew to race, and she was a second-hand boat. By now he knew exactly what he wanted in his own boat, one designed and built expressly for him, and the *Finisterre* project took shape in the early 50s.

It became almost the nautical equivalent of Babe Ruth pointing to the spot in the Wrigley Field stands where he was going to hit a homer, and then planting the ball there on the next pitch in the 1932 World Series.

By putting his ideas on paper in advance articles, and admitting that he was hoping to win races with his new brain child, Mitchell opened himself wide to the consequences of publicized failure. That he produced a success under the circumstances has become one of the legends of the sport. How he did it is an interesting study of the anatomy of a yachting winner, and it is also dated in time. *Finisterre* was a product of a new era, and the forerunner of much that came after. She came at the end of the era of wooden boats, the beginning of the era of synthetic sails, and ahead of certain changes in the rules that would tend to reduce the success of her type. That she was so successful was one of the reasons for these rule changes. She also marked the peak of custom yacht development. Soon afterward, stock boats began to take over.

Her name came first. Approaching Europe in a Transatlantic passage on *Caribbee*, Mitchell's eye was continually drawn on the chart to the bold cape at the northwestern corner of the Iberian peninsula. The music of the name *Finisterre*, and its significance—land's end—grew on him as he studied the charts, and he picked it then and there as the name of his dream child.

After a great deal of thinking, analysis, talk, comparison, study of other boats and reviewing of experience, he was ready to talk to Olin Stephens about a boat that really seemed a case of "having your cake and eating it too." He wanted her to be small enough for single-handed day sailing, comfortable enough for luxurious cruising with a small, congenial crew, able enough to cross oceans, fast enough to win races, and large enough to carry a tremendous load of luxury amenities such as mechanical refrigeration, all the available electronic aids to navigation, and fuel and water for extended passages. This ended up as a beamy, ballasted centerboarder, with her center of flotation well aft to keep her from squatting under the load of gear aboard, husky, strong, of premium construction, yawl-rigged for a combination of ease of handling and racing versatility. Stephens, not a man to make radical changes in one fell swoop, was a bit taken aback at some of the demands of the combination, but they were worked out, and Seth Persson of Saybrook, Conn., a "one-man" shop specializing in traditional quality, was chosen as the builder. She was finished in 1954, too late for the Bermuda Race of that year, and Mitchell spent long hours in seeing that everything aboard her suited him to perfection.

A plywood mockup had been built to test every detail of her arrangements and cabin plan, and, after hours of study and minor changes, it proved extremely valuable in that the finished boat was comfortable to cook in, sit in, sleep in and move around in. The only item that hadn't worked out to perfection was access to the auxiliary engine, which had been planned properly, but without allowance for the maze of pipes and wires that had to criss-cross the compartment to handle all the auxiliary gear.

Mitch took her south her first winter for the S.O.R.C., just then beginning to emerge as a great winter "World Series" of yachting,

Finisterre under full sail off Nassau

The Bermuda Trophy—
she won it three times

Carleton Mitchell

Winning 1958 Bermuda Race

attracting topnotch boats and sailors from all the most active areas.

The home-run ball took a good start toward the grandstand when *Finisterre* won her first start, the Fort Lauderdale-Bimini Race. She also won the Nassau Cup and was second in the two long races, Miami-Nassau and St. Pete-Havana, putting her second for the series. She performed well on all points of sailing, and later proved out her cruising capabilities with some gunkholing through the Bahamas.

The next winter she was back and went all the way, taking the S.O.R.C. series championship by finishing it with a win in the St. Pete-Havana Race.

The S.O.R.C. had proved invaluable, in the same way that it has for so many other boats in the years since, in bringing *Finisterre* to topnotch form. As on so many other S.O.R.C. entrants, boatless skippers of vast skill and experience from all over the world were delighted to sign on as crew.

So she could hardly be called an unknown boat when the squat gray yawl faced the starting gun at Brenton Reef Lightvessel on June 16, 1956. There was a record eighty-nine-boat fleet out on a gray, flat day, a jump of twelve in the entry list over 1954, and a new record in the twentieth holding of this number-one blue-water classic. A big spectator fleet was out to see the excitement, but there was very little of it, or of what was to come in the race, when the starting guns, boomed at 15-minute intervals for the four classes from the committee boat, U.S.S. *Rhodes*. The wind was a mild 8 knots for the big Class A boats, and they got away cleanly, but it pooped over an oily, flat sea soon afterward, and the rest of the classes were barely able to move forward. In fact, when it came the turn of Class D, most of them, including *Finisterre*, were drifting ignominiously backward toward the Rhode Island coast. Finally a moderate southwester filled in again and the boats began to inch toward the hazy, indistinct seaward horizon.

Fortified by his S.O.R.C. experience, Mitchell had *Finisterre* in absolute top shape in every respect. No ocean racer, at least up to that time, had ever been outfitted with more meticulous care. Her sails had been tested and proved effective in the southern racing, and those that didn't seem quite right had been replaced. This was an era in which some were still sticking to cotton for some sail use, but *Finisterre* had the most modern Dacron and nylon material for all of hers.

Not only had every piece of equipment been selected with the greatest care, with anything that had not proved completely satisfactory in the S.O.R.C. scrapped and replaced, but her crew had also been put together with great thought and a hard-nosed determination to have only the best. The experience of having all topnotch "chiefs" and no "Indians" aboard in the southern circuit had proved to Mitchell the extreme value of continuously skilled helmsmanship in getting the most out of a boat. "Why," he once said, "spend all that money on fancy gear and equipment to save you a few seconds per mile, and then put a man on the wheel who gives away minutes?"

With him for the race, already all familiar with the boat from previous racing down south, were Ned Freeman, Bunny Rigg, Corwith Cramer, Jr., Dick Bertram, Woody Pirie and a professional. Mitchell and Cramer shared the navigating, and everyone on board had a reputation as a skilled racing man and helmsman, which wasn't hurt in the future through having been part of *Finisterre's* crack bunch. With only a couple of changes, this crew stayed with her in her major races.

Stanley Rosenfeld, the well-known and extremely knowledgeable marine photographer, who followed in the footsteps of his father Morris as one of the few photographers whose presence nearby doesn't bother sailors because of their reputation for knowing what they're doing, tells an interesting anecdote of photographing *Finisterre* soon after the start of a Bermuda Race. As the Rosenfeld's famous launch *Foto*, with Stanley's brother William at the wheel, maneuvered under *Finisterre's* leeward quarter, always a favorite spot for good camera angles while being nautically safe, Stan began to feel that something was different. At first he couldn't latch onto the reason for the sensation, but suddenly he realized that there was a complete absence of the "creak-creak" noise *Foto's* steering gear usually made while she was being held at just the right distance and angle for good pictures.

Normally, William had to do a lot of steering while the sailboat subject of the moment yawed and wandered along, but *Finisterre* was sailing straight and true, in the groove, without a single wasteful wiggle of extra distance or rudder pressure to keep her from getting to Bermuda fast. Certainly this was part of her secret.

It didn't take long for that 1956 race to recover from its unmemorable start and develop into one of the most exciting and interesting of all the ones that have made it a legendary part of the sport. The southwester played over the fleet fitfully for about six hours, and then it began to fill in with more authority, until it was pumping a typical squally, smokey breeze of over 20 knots across the course. The fleet settled down for the expected starboard tack thrash, and the big boats really began to move.

So did *Finisterre*, driving hard, standing up well and staying up with bigger boats. Her navigation was letter-perfect as she didn't waste a mile in the cloudy, overcast going.

Whether she could have saved her time on the big 70-footers like *Bolero* and *Venturer* if this weather pattern had held all the way to the island is problematical. It was big-boat weather, and the two dark-hulled beauties from Olin Stephens's design board staged a thrilling duel that resulted in *Bolero* setting the course record of just over 70 hours as they charged into the finish line in a welter of heavy rain squalls that made navigation tricky and caused them to reduce sail near the finish.

But the Bermuda High, the typical weather pattern that settles over the area in early summer and pumps the return circulation of southwest air around its western edge, didn't hold for the little boats. A cold front was charging down from the continent in a southeasterly direction, gradually overtaking the boats. The author, covering the race from a Coast Guard patrol plane on Tuesday, June 19, had a graphic view of how the weather was developing.

As we took off from Great Sound, Bermuda, in teeming rain and strong southwesterly gusts, we soon picked up *Bolero* and *Venturer*.

They were less than 50 miles away at 0800, almost even and less than a mile apart, plunging powerfully over a steep chop, their lee rails awash and large sections of their underbodies exposed to the view from the sky. As we flew northwestward beyond them, the wind was easing off, and each boat we came to was in lighter going, until we began to find some about 100 miles out who were almost becalmed in patchy sunlight, trying to make spinnakers stay full in fitful catspaws.

They couldn't see, but we could, from a couple of thousand feet up, that the front we had been shown on the Air Station's weather map that morning was charging down on them like a dark, moving cliff. As we neared it, it seemed to have the solidity of a stone wall, towering out of sight above us and stretching ragged fingers down to the surface of the water. Suddenly we were in it, like going into a darkened room, and windy rain lashed at the plane, tossing it and shaking it in quick fury.

In only a few minutes of flying we burst out into gray daylight on the other side, with the rain gone, a high overcast far above us and the bleak, gray-blue sea below us lashed by whitecaps and windstreaks under a strong northeaster swirling in behind the front. For a while nothing but tossing wavetops could be seen, but then, amid the flicker, surge and fade of the tumbling whitecaps, we picked out a steady streak of white that didn't blend back into the blue. It was a boat, roaring along with a broad wake fanning astern, and we circled down to identify her. As we banked steeply and zoomed around, the number 260 could be seen on the mainsail, and everyone on the plane raised eyebrows when we checked the identification sheet and made sure she was *Finisterre*. She was standing stiffly and really making knots under full main and mizzen and a good-sized jib, surfing along with the breaking crests and looking very much in control of the situation. As one of the smallest and lowest-rating boats in the big fleet, she was far ahead of where any boat that size could be expected to be, and we all tabbed her immediately as the sure winner. Actually she was in the process of putting a remarkable day's run of 206 miles together, and all she needed was for the wind to hold. It did, and she swept in before it to finish just 20 hours and 15 minutes after *Bolero* early the next morning for a corrected time of 64 hours.

The ball had landed in the grandstand, but, as it turned out, that was only the beginning. It was remarkable enough to have her fulfill her owner's stated plans and ambitions so thoroughly, but to go on for three straight wins in this largest of all nautical games is a truly rare feat. Any boat that wins the Bermuda Race once has to be good. To win it three times she has to have some elements of luck, but she also has to be very good indeed, and this is why *Finisterre* has made such an impression on yachtsmen everywhere.

If luck could be said to enter into it, the 1958 race could be called the spot where it did. This was a classic small boat race, in which the weather pattern played right into the hands of the lowest-rating boats. The scratch sheet was virtually turned upside down in the corrected finish order, and *Finisterre* was right at the bottom of it. This was a case of the Bermuda High settling the great big calm spot at its center right over the finish area, just as the big boats arrived in the vicinity. They wallowed there while the small boats kept on coming in the circulation outside of the center that was still blowing across the course further up the rhumb line. They arrived along with a system of squalls, and virtually the whole fleet poured across the finish in a few wild, wet nighttime hours. The other memorable feature of the race was the start, the hairiest in its history, when the 111-boat fleet was dusted by a northwester that was steadily in the high 20s and had puffs well over 40.

The action was spectacular as spinnakers whanged in the sharp gusts, and boats broached in all directions, glistening underbodies turned to the bright sunlight, but *Finisterre* swept across under complete control and was in the right spot at the right time all through the race, taking her luck where she found it.

It was more than luck that brought her through the calms and storms of the 1960 race. She had good luck, but she was also superbly handled when the storm hit. Until then, she had not been in a commanding position. With all the replicas, near-sisters and "improvements" of her in the fleet, the competition was bound to be tougher, and almost every boat had a story that started "We were way ahead of *Finisterre* before that storm hit—we had her tucked away," when the race was being rehashed in Bermuda.

Through the worst of the storm, which started on Wednesday night, she was driven off on starboard tack, avoiding the mistake of

She was successful in the S.O.R.C.

some boats whose crews thought it was important to stay to the westward. The estimate of the weather pattern made on *Finisterre* was that the wind would gradually fair around to the west and northwest as the storm center passed, which it did, so she was not pinched, but was kept moving, with sail reduced by changing jibs and reefing the main as the wind increased, in a semicircular course to the eastward, gradually heading back for Bermuda as the wind faired around. This kept her speed up and gave her a better point of sailing on the approach to the finish.

And so there she was, in the bright Bermuda sunshine of Friday morning, back at the same position of honor at anchor in front of Royal Bermuda Yacht Club that she had occupied in 1956 and 1958. As she rode there jauntily with her pale gray topsides taking on some of the colorful hues of the water and sky, her brightwork glistening, and her ensign and burgees snapping in the breeze, she was a legend personified, a boat that had truly made her mark as one of the great ones.

Her beamy hull could handle a blow well

16

Chanticleer

In the tax-conscious 1960s, a yachting "grand tour" of Europe in the style of Commodore Vanderbilt's *North Star* cruise or the madcap junket of *Cleopatra's Barge* would seem almost as difficult a feat as those pioneer voyages were, for entirely different reasons. A yacht was the most comfortable way to travel when *North Star* and the *Barge* were making the rounds of European resorts, but the jet age and the era of luxury cruises on ocean liners changed all that.

There was plenty of long voyaging in yachts in the 60s, but most of it was in small sailboats, with adventurous souls eschewing the delights and comforts of civilization. Turning to a primitive contest with nature, they rounded the globe single-handed or took off as married couples or families to the exotic ports of the Caribbean, the South Seas and the Mediterranean. But a yachting cruise in the grand manner in a luxury vessel capable of crossing open oceans had become a distinct rarity.

First of all, there weren't that many big yachts any more, and most of them that were in commission spent much of their time moored stern-to the quay in some glamorous Mediterranean or Aegean port as a floating base for parties. Few American yachts were big enough to venture abroad in comfort. A 70- to 90-footer of the type classed as luxury yachts after World War II might seem big alongside stock

Chanticleer, a Defoe diesel yacht

cruisers in a marina, but she would suddenly seem a small little craft on the vast reaches of the open Atlantic or Pacific.

Ralph Evinrude had different ideas about using his 118-foot yacht *Chanticleer*, however. Bearing one of the most famous names in the pleasure-boat field, the son of the man who developed one of the first outboard motors and then built a company that manufactured it into an industry leader, is a true boatman, a lover of the sea, of boats as operating mechanisms, and of the fun and adventure of living aboard and using them.

Evinrude bought the steel-hulled yacht, built by DeFoe in 1947 at Bay City, Mich., in 1953, and began to use her extensively for North American cruising. With his wife, the former movie star Frances Langford, who became one of the most famous entertainers of her time in her many trips to entertain G.I.s in the war zones in World War II, Evinrude covered every major cruising area. The slender vessel with white superstructure, raking stack and royal blue hull, was a familiar sight all up and down the eastern seaboard between Nova Scotia and the Gulf of Mexico. She also was a frequent visitor to the St. Lawrence, the Great Lakes, the Mississippi River system and the Caribbean, and she had gone as far as Los Angeles on the West Coast, via the Panama Canal.

Although luxuriously fitted, with extra touches such as a complicated console that provided selected music to every cabin, *Chanticleer* was not just an elaborate platform for a party, as are many of the relatively few vessels her size. She was intended for long periods of comfortable living afloat, and many a dweller in a high-priced city apartment would have been goggle-eyed at her appointments.

Evinrude, an engineer by training and inclination, also had the time of his life making sure that everything about her mechanical features was as good as could be found. For power she had four GM six-cylinder 671 diesels with a cylinder displacement of 71 cubic inches and rated at 180 hp. at 1,800 r.p.m. This meant a cruising speed of 14 knots, with the four engines operating two shafts and two propellers, which burned about 35 g.p.h. including operation of one 30 kw. generator. Of these, she had two 371 GMs, and they ran in an engineroom sound-proofed by research engineers from Evinrude's company, Outboard Marine Corp., using sound-deadening techniques that had been one of the big factors in bringing outboard motors to such booming popularity in the 1950s.

Her pilot house contained every electronic device known to man that could be of help in operating a vessel of her size. Automatic pilot, radar, loran, depth-sounder, radiotelephone and every kind of safety alarm, plus engine controls, all gleaming and shining without a fingerprint on them, gave her bridge the look of a modern ocean liner. The pilot house was unusually spacious, because Evinrude delighted in showing his guests the operation of the vessel while she was under way, and gone were the days when the enormous crews needed to run a steam yacht lived and slept in rabbit warren forecastles deep in the forepeak. *Chanticleer's* crew, large by modern standards with eight men in it, had the use of this big airy house as a lounge while in port.

Evinrude, a large, round, balding man with a boyish sense of humor, loved showing visitors all of this, and he also had favorite gags and gimmicks, like a picture of a nude girl sitting in the radar scope, which he would light up after getting guests seriously prepared for a demonstration of radar's technical marvels.

Chanticleer was later fitted with two more features that set her apart from most yachts. Anti-roll stabilizing fins, hydraulically controlled and retractable, cut her rolling in a beam sea from as much as 30° to only 3°, and she was also equipped with bow jets. Valves at the bow underwater could be controlled from the bridge to shoot 1,000 gallons per minute at 80 pounds of pressure. The jet was operated by disconnecting one of the four main engines from the propeller shaft and hitching it to pumps for the jets. By combining use of her twin screws and these jets, the long, slender vessel could virtually be moved sideways into a tight-fitting berth, and could also be backed and handled around slips and in close quarters with great maneuverability.

Naturally her ship's boats were the latest products from OMC's boat-building operations, plus smaller launches equipped with outboard motors, and these alone were enough to make the average boatlover drool covetously.

In all her operations, *Chanticleer* was really used as a boat. For weeks at a time, the Evinrudes, with perhaps a few close friends, would take her to isolated harbors in Lake Huron's North Channel or somewhere in the Florida Keys, but then she would show up for important yachting events like the America's Cup to take guests out for the spectacle. In New York, it wasn't an unusual sight to see her moored off the Seventy-ninth Street Yacht Basin in the Hudson River while her launches brought out boatloads of friends from Frances's show business days, including Jerry Colonna rolling his eyes and twitching his moustache amid a bevy of Copa girls, or musicians who had played for her on her many tours.

Sometimes Evinrude used the yacht to call on dealer marinas so that OMC products could be demonstrated, a fairly impressive way of making a business call.

Through all this extensive and very pleasant use, and as he got to know her better and better, Evinrude began to build a dream of wider oceans to conquer. Often, visitors, awed by *Chanticleer's* size, would ask whether she could cross the ocean, and the answer was that she could, but hadn't done it. More and more this began to seem like a good idea, until finally it became almost an obsessive challenge. One by one, difficulties and objections were analyzed and disposed of, and by late 1964, the decision was made to start planning a cruise from *Chanticleer's* home base at Stuart, Fla., to the Mediterranean and return.

From January on, Evinrude, his captain, John Robinson, and the rest of the crew worked to get *Chanticleer* ready for the voyage. The Captain studied wind and weather charts for the best average conditions and picked June 15 as the starting date. The boat was given a complete overhaul, and her fuel capacity was increased to 6,000 gallons by converting one of her water tanks, since her watermaker could provide 550 gallons per day. Extra drums were lashed on deck, an extra radiotelephone was installed, and two fifteen-man liferafts were added. Once inflated, they were practically little luxury yachts themselves, but they made the trip in cylindrical containers each about the size of a 55 gallon drum. They would automatically disengage themselves at a depth of 15 feet and would then inflate, if they ended up in the water. Other special touches included plywood panels

Ralph Evinrude and his wife, movie star Frances Langford, aboard *Chanticleer*

Evinrude checks the galley fare

Frances Langford Evinrude in the dining saloon

for all the deckhouse windows, a second navigator to assist the captain, and enough food for a month.

In addition to the professional crew, the ship's company included the Evinrudes, Frances's friend Patty Thomas, who had traveled extensively with her throughout the South Pacific with the Bob Hope troupe, and ChiChi Gonzolus, a registered nurse whose husband was the family's doctor. Two seagoing poodles completed the entourage for the Transatlantic crossing.

The voyage was a monument to good planning and good execution. In a voyage of this scope, so many things could go wrong, and so many well-laid plans could turn into fiascos, but there were no horror tales to tell, except for *Chanticleer's* reception in Egypt.

The run to Bermuda took three days. Fresh food was taken on, the tanks were topped, and on June 20 the longest open-water leg, eight days to the Azores, was started under a bright blue Bermuda sky. Good weather held all the way. The seas were completely smooth, and it was a pleasant rest cruise for those on board. The ship's four TV sets lost mainland programs 150 miles out, and were only good for pictures, not sound, once in Eurpoe, but there was a stock of Hollywood movies on board, and short wave radio brought in the Voice of America and Armed Forces Radio. A few ships passed en route caused a flurry of excitement.

A short stop in the Azores brought a chance for more re-supply activity and the small boats were used to explore the beaches and coves of the mountainous islands. From here it was three and a half days to Gibraltar, where more guests came aboard, and the cruise really began to assume "grand tour" proportions.

Majorca, Minorca, Barcelona, the Riviera, Portofino and Elba were stopping places on the way to a planned break at Naples. The crew became adept at squeezing *Chanticleer's* 18-foot 5-inch beam into slots that seemed quite a bit narrower, using the "everybody push" method, and a specially built stern gangplank and winch, installed for the cruise, made going ashore easy in the Mediterranean fashion of tying stern-to the quay. No other method is possible in the small, jampacked harbors, and absence of tidal rise and fall makes the practice feasible.

From Naples, Evinrude flew back to the States for business meetings, while the three ladies of the *Chanticleer* took off on a motor tour of the Continent. In a gesture that might have surprised the nabobs who took their yachts to Europe in the palmy pre-World War I days, Evinrude had the wives of the six married crew members flown to Naples from the United States for the three weeks the vessel was tied up there.

When the cruise started again on August 18, *Chanticleer* went south to Sicily, and Frances, still as trim and svelte as when she visited them in World War II, could note the vast differences in Palermo and Messina since she had seen them bombed out in the darker days of the war.

Heading across to the Greek island of Corfu, there was embarrassing contretemps there when Evinrude, having seen a fleet of American-built launches and small powerboats moored in an attractive cove as *Chanticleer* ranged by on her way to an anchorage, came back by small boat to have a look. Instead of being welcomed, he was waved away violently, but not before shouting out what he thought of this treatment of visiting yachtsmen. Later, he found that this was the private cove of King Constantine's summer palace, and he had tried to force his way in at the height of the political crises with Prime Minister Papandreou, when the Navy guarding the King's cove was a mite nervous about strange vessels approaching.

Continuing on in a cruise rare in the annals of modern American yachting, *Chanticleer* poked her blue bow into the mountain-girt Gulf of Corinth and through the high-sided Corinth Canal to Piraeus, then on through the Aegean Islands to Istanbul, where she became the first American vessel to enter the Black Sea in several years, and spent a quiet afternoon with her company swimming and fishing over the side. A swinging party for U.S. Navy Sixth Fleet officers livened the Istanbul stay, although Evinrude at first thought he had a load of crashers when the first boatload arrived wearing sport clothes and turned out to be admirals.

Stops at Lesbos, Samos and glittering Rhodes led to the only real misadventure of the cruise, a decision to visit Egypt even without visas or landing permits.

Chanticleer's diesel engines

Though not exactly a disaster, this was an ill-advised move, as the Egyptians were surly and uncooperative, kept everyone aboard for 24 hours, and then posted guards on board to check all comings and goings. On advice of a shipping agent, Evinrude hired guards to guard the guards, and then set his own crew to guard the guards who were guarding the guards. This Gilbert and Sullivan-like situation was the background for a three-flat tire trip to Cairo in a rented Cadillac that had had its engine replaced by a four-cylinder diesel, but, after a night of listening to depth bombings in the harbor by Egyptian patrol boats looking for Israeli saboteurs, everyone was glad to set sail. Not, however, until after paying port charges of $400.

The voyage home was smooth and relatively uneventful, with a stop at the good shipyard facilities on Malta, a growing yachting center, for a haulout and bottom painting. The return route led along the African Coast to Gibraltar again, and then southward in the Atlantic via Casablanca and the Canaries to Dakar. The only rough weather of the cruise hit *Chanticleer* between Casablanca and the Canaries, but the stabilizers kept her relatively comfortable if she was held to under 10 knots. From Dakar and its colorful bazaars and lush, tropical vegetation, a run to the Cape Verde islands, lonely and barren, for final fuel and provisions, set the stage for the long leg of the return crossing, eight days on the twelfth parallel to Barbados.

This was another quiet crossing, starting on October 25, after the hurricane season had virtually ended. Not a ship was seen, but the newly discovered Ikeya-Seki comet loomed like a searchlight beam on the southeast horizon every night of the passage, and squads of flying fish flopped onto the deck at night, lured to their fate by *Chanticleer's* bright cabin lights. Barbados came up over the starboard bow on schedule, and the rest of the cruise was one that other yachts have followed more often than the previous portions of it, through the Lesser and Greater Antilles and the Bahamas to home base at Stuart, which was reached on November 21.

Chanticleer's cruise showed that yachting in the grand style, despite all the changes in it, had not completely departed from the American scene by the mid 1960s, but it was almost the exception that proved the rule.

Intrepid in action

17

Intrepid

Every America's Cup defender creates her own set of legends. Just by winning in this most rarefied of all nautical competitions she becomes a great yacht in her own right, but, like *Ranger* as the superboat of the J era, there can be an extra something to set a certain boat apart, even from her illustrious sisters.

Intrepid has it, for a special combination of reasons. In 1967 she had held, like *Ranger* thirty years previously, complete mastery both over her American rivals and the challenger. She was perfection afloat, commanding respect not so much from affection or emotion, but rather through appreciation of the sheer overwhelming superiority of her performance. She had that cachet that goes with a truly outstanding champion, and this was enough to earn her a special niche in the history of yachts that have become legendary.

But then she added another chapter, this time in an entirely new vein. She did what only one previous defender had ever done in Cup history. She repeated her role, but the story was a very different one in 1970. While the 1967 campaign had been a coldly efficient devastation of all opposition in which the only drama lay in the continuity of perfection, her second defense was an exciting cliff-hanger. In it was packed just about as much excitement, controversy and suspenseful battling as in all the twenty previous defenses.

Set apart by this unusual contrast in her two campaigns, she deserves her rating as the great Cup yacht of the modern era, and her story is an interesting testament to the demands and pressures of achieving success in this unique competition.

Only the world of yachting knows or cares who wins a Bermuda Race or Transpac, an Olympic medal, or a class championship, but all the world knows about the America's Cup, and this creates fantastic extra pressures. What other sport can bring forth the expenditure of several million dollars in one season to produce four wins by one competitor over another, with no thought whatsoever of any financial return on any part of the outlay?

In most sailing, the time actually spent in competition is far greater than the time spent in training. Only a few dedicated one-design sailors with Olympic ambitions spend long hours in practice drills, but the America's Cup competition is a dramatic exception. Because of the tremendous pressure to win in virtually the only sailboat event that consists solely of match racing, and because of the intense competition to gain the defender's berth, this is sailing in deadly earnest. No hopping aboard from the club launch 15 minutes before the gun, and then back to the bar the minute the race is over.

When the competition was revived in 1958 by changing the deed of gift for the cup *America* brought home in 1851, making it possible to use 12-Meter sloops that did not have to be sailed across the ocean on their own bottom, it opened an era that was quite different from the J-boat campaigns of the 1930s. They ended with *Ranger's* smashing success.

In the J-boat days, there were long hours of practice, but the atmosphere was quite different. The professional crews of about thirty men were not giving up time from shore jobs, or from a college vacation. This was their job, and the four or five gentlemen of the afterguard were usually of a financial standing which caused them no hardship to take the summer off to go sailing. Drills were earnest, and long hours were spent in perfecting gear and techniques, but there was still no comparison to the summer-long pressure-cooker that campaigning a 12-Meter for the America's Cup had become by the time the 1967 build-up started.

There were no longer any professional sailors who were qualified to man a modern racing machine. All the talent had to be recruited from the ranks of amateur, but eager, volunteers. Hopefuls could be carefully screened to pick out the best. Because eleven men were required as crew of the 65-foot-long sloops, there was an obvious analogy to a football team, and a good crew needed a not dissimilar combination of brains, leadership, speed, dexterity, and sheer brawn. Once assembled, it was then put through as rigorous a season of preparation and training as any football or other championship team ever had. Since it consisted of amateurs who did this because they wanted to and for the glory of it, the intensity of dedication of a 12-Meter crew generally far outstripped any other type of training or preparation for sailing competition.

Although they lived in regal splendor in lavish "cottages" rented for the season at Newport, R.I., where the trials and races are held, the atmosphere was actually closer to that of a training camp or barracks. Would-be playboys soon found they couldn't mix much Newport social life with the training regimen, and even married crew members had to have wives who were understanding and patient under long days of neglect and early evening curfews.

The boats were treated with the same intense dedication, which meant slavish attention to each detail, no matter how tiny, and a constant striving for perfection in design, rig, gear and sails with cost no object. By the mid-60s, a properly mounted program to build and campaign a Cup defender meant an outlay of about a million dollars, with no tax relief and only a minor return on eventual sale of the boat.

This was the situation when the Royal Sydney Yacht Squadron put in a challenge for 1967. The Australians had thrown a scare into the New York Yacht Club by mounting a dangerous challenge in 1962, and the news that they were coming back again, challenging right after the dismal British failure in the 1964 series, started wheels turning in the membership.

The usual rumors were whispered across the white tablecloths of the club's heavy-beamed grill room, and a casual luncheon between two people known to have some interest in the Cup's defense could start a whole new batch. Naval architects sat anxiously by their telephones waiting for the right call, but once the phone rang in the plain, utilitarian office of Olin Stephens in the design section of his firm, Sparkman & Stephens, on lower Madison Avenue in New York, the rumors, and the hopeful expectancy in other offices, died down like a brush fire in a thundersquall.

The call was from William Strawbridge of the Philadelphia department store family, who had been working on forming a syndicate after gaining experience with *American Eagle* in the 1964 campaign. It had been like putting a very expensive jigsaw puzzle together, a puzzle in which the pieces had to lock independently and with proper timing. Strawbridge wanted Olin Stephens as the designer, Bus Mosbacher, whose masterful helmsmanship had been the key to *Weatherly's* success against the first Aussie challenge in 1962, as skipper, and, of course, backers with money. He had ex-Commodore Burr Bartram, but he needed more. Each element needed assurance that the other elements were also present, in a nautical version of "After you, Alphonse," but Strawbridge finally tied the package together. The key to it was a personal visit he, Mosbacher, Stephens, and Bartram made to the grand old man of the club, Harold S. Vanderbilt. "Mike" Vanderbilt, in his 80's and no longer robust, still had a keen interest in the defense of the Cup he had won three times, and when he said he would join the syndicate, it was a virtual go-ahead signal. Mosbacher had left himself a possible out because of the pressure of family business, and it became a family joke. Even after the campaign had ended, his wife Pat would ask, "When are you going to give the syndicate a definite yes?" But he couldn't resist the combination of working for the first time with Stephens on a new design. He had sailed on the revamped *Vim*, a 1939 Stephens boat, against the new Stephens design, *Columbia*, in 1958, as well as on *Weatherly*, which Phil Rhodes had designed in 1958.

When this syndicate was announced, along with the word that Stephens would consult with anyone campaigning his former creations, *Columbia* (1958) and *Constellation* (1964), but would only design one boat, all other tentative plans for new boats that had been hatching in New York, Detroit, Southern California and Florida died quick-

Bus Mosbacher, her 1967 skipper

The controlled bend in her
titanium-topped mast

ly. No one wanted to bet a million dollars against the combination of Stephens, Mosbacher, Vanderbilt and the other knowledgeable gentlemen of the Intrepid Syndicate.

And so the rumors switched from "who?" to "what?" What would Stephens do to top his superb brainchild *Constellation*, the runaway victor over *Sovereign* in 1964? Some had termed *Connie* a "breakthrough" even though she had a tough time, finally coming from behind against *American Eagle* in the trials after Bob Bavier had taken over her helm, but Stephens scoffed at this designation. In the fall of 1964 he had said he was sure she could be improved upon, which raised the fascinating question—how?

There was no way of knowing for quite a while. Wrapped in security that would have done credit to the Manhattan Project, the new boat was taking shape behind closed doors at the Minneford yard on City Island, at the western end of Long Island Sound. Stephens had been emphasizing reduced wetted surface and separation of rudder and keel in his recent ocean racing designs, and there was continuous conjecture on how he would apply this thinking to the new Cup yacht.

A British journalist broke a release date and published material a month early amid cries of "foul" and fears that the Aussies would have time to copy some of the elements, but actually Warwick Hood, who was designing *Dame Pattie*, the Australian challenger, had a pretty good idea of Stephen's intentions even before seeing the material in the jumped release. When I visited his office in Sydney in March 1967, he was able to sketch a remarkably accurate facsimile of *Intrepid's* profile based on his knowledge of what Stephens had been doing with other new designs.

When *Intrepid* was launched in May, there were still some surprises, however. As she slid down the ways, there was a canvas cover over her deck, hiding two large bulges at the usual spots for coffee-grinder winches. Eventually it was revealed that the bulges were G.I. cans and that the coffee grinders, in a radical move worked out in consultation by Mosbacher and Stephens, had been placed below decks. The weight of the winches and the muscle men to operate them would be located as low as possible, an important factor in stability and saving of weight topsides.

No visitors were allowed below decks until well on in the campaign, but her underbody, featuring a short keel, separate rudder, with a skeg connecting it to the keel, and a trim tab on the keel had been revealed, and immediately, *Dame Pattie* and the other defense candidates, the re-treads *American Eagle, Constellation* and *Columbia*, all began to sprout "bustles" in some form or other on their underbodies.

As soon as *Intrepid* began sailing, however, it was apparent that little could be done by her competitors to catch up with the sum total of advances she represented. Not only did she have a new (for 12-Meters) underwater shape and a radically new winch set-up. She also had extremely sophisticated advances in rigging, including a titanium top to her mainmast to improve its bending qualities, a rod headstay and the most advanced spinnaker-handling gear. To go with her underwater innovations, the trimming rudder on the keel and the main rudder in its separated position aft were controlled by a complicated double wheel with clutches, and the proper use of them in combination enhanced her turning ability and even her ability to slow down when necessary. With both rudders working together, she could turn inside any other Twelve, and when they were set against each other, they had a braking effect, sometimes a valuable asset in the quick turns and maneuvers just before the start of a match race.

Her sails, turned out by sailmaker Ted Hood of Marblehead, Mass., who had established a complete corner on 12-Meter sails over the past three campaigns, took advantage of new developments in sailcloth and weaving so that they could be of much lighter cloth than in previous campaigns, 7-ounce weight for a mainsail as opposed to a previous standard of 12-ounce, and still hold their shape in all conditions.

Intrepid not only had the latest in design, rig and sailmaking. She also had one of the best crews ever assembled, attracted by the opportunity to sail with Mosbacher, a cool, smooth competitor who had forged his talents in the intensely competitive International One-Design Class on Long Island Sound before tackling 12-Meters in 1958. By 1967, he had more hours on the wheel of a 12-Meter in competition than anyone else sailing, and he knew exactly what was required in the way of a crew and the organization of it. In all his sailing career, Mosbacher had been under extra pressure to be right and to do the right thing, as, by his own force of personality, fine sportsmanship, impeccable handling of any and all competitive crises, and gentlemanly behavior, he had been one of the first Jewish sailors to break some of the barriers of a world that was finally coming out of a cocoon of exclusivity and hidebound prejudice. Everybody wanted to sail with Bus, and he picked a crack crew out of the many hopefuls.

Everything fell together very quickly, and *Intrepid* was obviously the boat to beat from the very first trial brush with *Connie*, which had been chartered back from her new European owners as a trial horse for *Intrepid*, a valuable yardstick to measure how Stephens's improvements were working out. *Connie* was also included in the trials as a candidate in case *Intrepid* failed to fulfill her promise, but there was never any question of that. Bob Bavier, who had been asked to sail his old love *Connie* in an early practice brush with *Intrepid*, came away shaking his head in amazement at *Intrepid's* maneuverability and quick acceleration.

In all the trial races she only lost one race, and that by a ludicrous navigation error that only proved that there was a human side to her imposing facade. While leading *Eagle* by a good margin in one of the June preliminaries on Long Island Sound, she rounded the wrong mark and blew the lead, and it was just about the only error that anyone could rib her crew about all year.

After this one lapse, she went on to completely dominate the summer. No matter how well-sailed *Eagle*, *Connie* and a revamped *Columbia* were, *Intrepid* made a shambles of every match race. Only in a fleet race on the New York Yacht Club cruise, with a record seven Twelves—*Intrepid*, *Columbia*, *Eagle*, *Connie*, *Nefertiti*, *Weatherly* and *Sceptre*—on the line, did *Intrepid*, hurt by a late start and a wind shift, fail to win. *Columbia* beat her, lending a measure of suspense to the resumption of match race trials in August, but Mosbacher quickly squelched any ideas of a change by carrying *Columbia* away from the starting line for three minutes after the gun in their first encounter, dumping her far back there, and then jibing away to forge a resounding victory.

Except in situations like this, he didn't even bother with the usual

During a practice sail. Low boom and winches below deck were innovations.

pre-start ring-around-a-rosy in-fighting that had added so much excitement to the previous campaigns. He just concentrated on keeping *Intrepid's* wind clear and letting her go. She would take over early on the first windward leg and that would be it. It was monotonous, but there was a certain fascination in the monotony of the excellence.

The inevitability of her superiority sank in on the Australians at an early date, and, although they put up a brave public front and even started a minor controversy or two, the fire and excitement of their 1962 challenge was absent. Then they had really believed, and rightfully so, that they had a fast boat with a chance, but this time they more or less went through the motions, waiting out a long summer in lonely practice sails as *Intrepid* swamped her American rivals.

Ten minutes of the first Cup race showed even the most optimistic Aussie of the hundreds who journeyed all the way to Newport to watch the series that *Dame Pattie*, though probably the second-best 12-Meter built up to that time, couldn't touch the American machine. After the series was over, it could be determined that *Intrepid's* time margins averaged out to about 11 seconds a mile, and she had begun to apply that edge right from the very first gun. Jock Sturrock, *Dame Pattie's* skipper, tried one little brush of pre-race maneuvering, and his jaw dropped open when he saw *Intrepid's* much smaller turning circle. Realizing there was no future in this kind of combat, he tamely went for what is called the safe leeward position, which is a fine place to be when you have a faster boat, but hopeless in a slower one. *Intrepid* had the lead, with her wind clear, by the first tack, and that was that.

The second start developed as a carbon copy of the first, and *Dame Pattie* gained a momentary edge when a header put *Intrepid* in her wake. Mosbacher tacked away first, an admission that he was at a disadvantage, but he had a two-length lead after holding this tack for 16 minutes, and crossed the *Dame's* bow. Here Sturrock pulled the desperate gamble of the trailing boat in a match race, a quick-tacking duel, but this soon backfired in a futile ruse, a false tack. Hanging in the wind, *Dame Pattie* lost all momentum, while Mosbacher refused to take the bait. After the merest flicker of hesitation in answer to Sturrock's feint, *Intrepid* drove off again on the same tack, leaping

She was virtually unbeatable in trials. Leading *American Eagle* here.

In action against *Dame Pattie, Intrepid* (leading) was stiffer and handled seas better. Note angle of heel of two boats.

several more lengths into the lead, and the only significant flurry of the series was over.

In the third race, Mosbacher's major obstacle was a helicopter rescuing two young men from a small sailboat that had been capsized by the chopper's down-blast while being warned off the course. Just in time *Intrepid*'s sheets were slacked and she bore off from the area of turbulence, or she might have been a victim of what would surely have been the most bizarre dismasting in sailboat racing history.

Warwick Hood had admittedly gambled that there would be light air off Newport, having studied the September statistics for a period of years, and his gamble had been foiled by a sparkling, clear three-day northeaster of 14-20 knots, imprisoned in the Rhode Island area by two oddly-behaved hurricanes further offshore. As it turned out, though, wind strength made little difference. A fog-shrouded fourth race sailed in a moderate southwester of under 12 knots was just as much to *Intrepid*'s liking as the heavy going, and she was far in the lead after the first tack.

And so she wrapped up one of the most decisive victories in all the one-sided triumphs of the America's Cup defense. Against an obviously well-sailed and well-designed challenger she had been invincible, and she could have been gracefully retired as another "super-boat" with her reputation secure.

In fact her syndicate might possibly have been warned off from any repeat effort by the fate of her historic namesake, the original U.S.S. *Intrepid*. She was a 60-foot, 4-gun ketch, just a bit shorter than a modern Twelve, which was captured by the U.S. Frigate *Constitution* and U.S. Schooner *Enterprise* off the Barbary Coast in 1803. When taken, she was a naval vessel from Tripoli named *Mastico*, but Captain Edward Preble of *Constitution* renamed her *Intrepid* and put Lieutenant Stephen Decatur, Jr. in command.

On February 16, 1804, Decatur took *Intrepid* into the harbor of Tripoli under the guns of forts and enemy ships and put her alongside the U.S. Frigate *Philadelphia*, which had been captured while aground at the harbor entrance. To prevent the frigate from being used against the American forces, Decatur set her afire and sank her and brought *Intrepid* out safely without the loss of a man.

Encounter with helicopter was biggest hazard of 1967 series

Her next venture was not as successful, however. Sent into the harbor of Tripoli as a fire ship to destroy enemy ships and installations she was discovered and was blown up prematurely with the loss of all hands, but with great damage to the forces of Tripoli.

Historic precedent meant little to the syndicate in 1970, however. Slightly revamped, with Vanderbilt having joined the rival Valiant Syndicate, and tugboat executive Briggs Dalzell in as a major new member, the *Intrepid* group, which had refused to accept foreign offers to buy her after her 1967 triumph, decided to campaign her again. They had also lost Olin Stephens, who had naturally been sought after to design a new boat and had signed with Bob McCullough's Valiant Syndicate. Sticking to his usual policy, Stephens would only work on one boat, and the question therefore arose as to whether he would once again improve on his previous creation, as he had done with *Columbia* (1958) over *Vim* (1939), *Constellation* (1964) over *Columbia*, and *Intrepid* (1967) over *Connie*.

The odds were that he would, and the Intrepid Syndicate therefore made the unusual move of tampering with a proven winner. Mosbacher, who had become Chief of Protocol for the State Department, would not be available, and there was an entirely new situation to face. As re-designer, they went to Britton Chance, Jr. a twenty-seven-year-old Philadelphian whose father had won the 5.5-Meter Olympic Gold Medal in 1952, and who had made quite a reputation for himself designing 5.5-Meters, a development class with many of the same problems and characteristics, in miniature, of their bigger 12-Meter sisters. Chance had also worked with Ted Hood on 12-Meter designs and had actually designed one 12-Meter on his own. A new element had entered the 1970 campaign, as the French had challenged as well as the Australians, and an agreement had been reached whereby the French and Aussies would sail off for the right to be the challenger. As part of the French preparatory campaign by Baron Marcel Bich, a ballpoint pen tycoon who was unknown in the yachting world until he was suddenly bitten by the America's Cup bug, Chance was signed to design a trial horse. She was built in Switzerland by Herman Egger and named *Chancegger*. The French had already acquired *Constellation*, *Sovereign*, and her sistership *Kurrewa*, for training purposes,

Intrepid was considerably altered for 1970. In June trials her paint job wasn't yet complete.

She handled *Heritage* easily in their trial races

and the new Chance design would also only be a trial boat, as the designer had to come from the challenging country, but working on it was valuable experience for the young designer.

Unabashed at the thought of altering the design of an acknowledged master, Chance stepped into the re-design of *Intrepid* confidently and began an intense tank-testing program. He was a bit late in starting, and financial and time considerations limited the amount of alterations he could make, so he concentrated on the after underbody and rig. The keel was shortened, the underbody sections were made fuller, ballast was increased, sail area slightly reduced, and many refinements were made in gear and equipment. New composite synthetics such as boron were used to lighten her boom, spinnaker pole and spreaders, and beryllium was used in the upper part of the mast to reduce weight there.

She was re-launched later than *Valiant* and *Heritage*, another new candidate that had been financed, designed and built by Charley Morgan of St. Petersburg, Fla., who was also to be her skipper, and the new underbody was shrouded in canvas tarps as she hit the water in City Island. Secrecy seemed part of the *Intrepid* tradition.

For its skipper, the syndicate went to a tall, confident Californian named Bill Ficker, an architect by profession with a world Star Class championship to his credit who had gotten the feel of a 12-Meter (and the America's Cup bug) while handling *Columbia* for some of her starts in 1967.

Ficker picked a young crew of muscular, quick one-design sailors with a minimum of 12-Meter experience, except for Steve Van Dyck, who had been on *Connie* in 1964 and had wide ocean racing experience. Van Dyck was to act as tactician, figuring out speed, courses, and other vital information from sophisticated dead reckoning equipment, while Ficker concentrated on boat speed and sail trim.

After a shaky start in the June trials on Long Island Sound, with much of her new gear not ready and the youngsters feeling their way toward the kind of effortless cooperation a Cup crew must have, *Intrepid* began to round into form in the July trials off Newport, but it was far from the clear sailing that 1967 had been. McCullough and *Valiant* had been the dominant factors in the Preliminary trials in

June, and it was obviously going to be a showdown between the new Stephens boat and his revamped 1967 winner. *Valiant* lost Vanderbilt's support with his death at eighty-five on July 4.

With suspense in every encounter, *Intrepid* and *Valiant* slugged it out through the summer, and gradually the older boat began to build up an edge of victories and of steadier performances. *Valiant*, probably the most sophsiticated racing machine ever built, was hard to handle in some conditions, and *Intrepid*, increasingly, was able to take her measure as all the new elements in her re-design began to jell. It was disturbing to all that the aging *Weatherly*, supposedly *Valiant's* trial horse, with experienced George Hinman as skipper, often gave the new boats fits in light air, but *Heritage* had not been able to find her potential.

Intrepid continued to improve, and she put a 9-1 string together in the August trials (22-5 in all the trials) to earn the selection as defender for a second time. The only other yacht ever to defend twice was *Columbia*, in 1899 and 1901. The final race, a hammer-and-tongs affair with *Valiant* in which *Intrepid* came from behind and went on to a 1:51 win, was one of the best of the summer, and it dramatized how different her task had been compared to 1967.

If the trials were that much more difficult, they were nothing compared to the battle she was to face in the Cup matches. Once again the Aussies had come up with a dangerous challenger. As he had for Sydney publisher Sir Frank Packer with *Gretel* in 1962, Alan Payne, in *Gretel II* had designed for Packer a fast, lively boat that had as much potential as any Twelve in existence. With champion small-boat sailor Jim Hardy as skipper, she easily disposed of Baron Bich's *France*, a near-copy of *Chancegger*, by a 4-0 score in a precedent-shattering elimination series off Newport in August, setting the stage for the twenty-first defense in 100 years of Cup history.

The series started Tuesday, September 15, with a cold, rainy easterly building a lump of sea over Rhode Island Sound as the boats were towed the seven miles out to the orange and white America's Cup buoy. *Intrepid's* pale green deck and *Gretel's* varnished one glistened in the rain and spray, and water streamed off the foul weather gear of the crews huddled in the cockpits, while the spectator fleet,

It was an uphill fight to catch *Valiant* in the trial series

perhaps 600 boats, took its lumps in the heavy going. The breeze was up to about 20 as the boats dropped their tows, hoisted mains and began to swoop in circles waiting for the starting signals. *Gretel*'s sail was a peculiar pale lavender, made of English Vectis cloth, and appeared to be as good a main as a 12-Meter challenger had shown so far.

The boats were moving virtually at hull speed under main alone, and tension seemed to wind up with each swift leap over the white-caps. Their first close approach came with about seven minutes to go. As they sped by on opposite tacks, there was a quick flurry of course changing, but no one noticed anything amiss. Then it could be seen that both were flying little red squares in their rigging. There had been a protest situation in that very first encounter. There had not been a protest in America's Cup competition since 1934.

As the starting time approached, *Gretel* took a position on *Intrepid*'s stern and had the American boat under control while they reached away from the line on port tack, but, when she broke off first and tacked away for the line with 1:38 to go, she was too early. Hardy had to bear off and drive down the line to leeward, while Ficker jibed and headed back for the windward end. He timed it just right, but Hardy was late in hardening up and lost more precious distance to leeward as they went off in a smother of flying spray with the gun with *Intrepid* on top. At first *Intrepid* appeared to be stiffer, while footing faster and pointing higher, and veteran spectators had that sinking feeling that this was going to be another walkover like 1958, 1964 or 1967.

How wrong they were. *Gretel* soon settled down and began to show equal speed with *Intrepid*, and they were off on one of the most incident-packed, controversy-fraught, exciting matches in the history of sailing. More "firsts" and more strange happenings popped up in this series than in any several combined, and it convincingly killed the old cliches about how dull it is to watch sailboat racing.

The protest, later to be overshadowed and almost forgotten, was enough of a surprise for a starter, but it was only a foretaste. *Intrepid* rounded the first mark with a lead of 1:03, and it could still be a race if *Gretel* should bring up a fresher breeze on the spinnaker reach.

A critical moment of the third race, with *Intrepid* jibing for mark at right moment while *Gretel* stands on port tack

What she brought up instead was a horrendous spinnaker wrap, the first in modern times, that lasted for six agonizing minutes. So close were the boats to hull speed, however, that she only dropped a few seconds on the leg, and there were still prospects of a real battle as they squared away for a reach, changing to genoas.

The Australian rooters—and there were many in the fleet strictly on sentiment as well as bona fide Aussies—already shaken by the wrap, were jolted again and harder when *Gretel* suddenly tacked back along her course, sails a-shiver, and those on the close-in spectator boats could see a head bobbing in the water. Paul Salmon, her foredeck man, had been lifted right off the deck when she put her bow through green water while he was returning from securing the spinnaker pole, and he had nothing to grab. A second pass and a delay of over three minutes finally saw him aboard, but any hope of a contest was ended. *Gretel* stayed even thereafter, but the margin was 5:52.

The protest, settled the next morning, which had been called as a lay day by the Aussies, was declared no foul as there had been no contact. *Gretel*, obviously seeking trouble, had protested *Intrepid* on a port-starboard situation, and *Intrepid* had counter-protested that *Gretel* had tried to obstruct her in the act of keeping clear. There was general surprise that the New York Yacht Club Race Committee was acting as its own protest committee in the series. This procedure had received little attention because of the lack of any protests since 1934, but it proved an unfortunate decision from a public relations point of view.

The second race, which took six days to become an official one, must go down, in all its ramifications, as perhaps the wildest sequence of events in America's Cup history. After the first race, there was the usual request for a lay day, permitted to either contestant after a race or an attempt at a race. The Aussies were the first ones to make the request, and, after this Wednesday layover, Thursday's attempt at a start before a mammoth fleet fell a victim of lack of wind. Friday was a gray, soggy day, and, with tension mounting each time the boats appeared, brought a few more startling developments.

First the Aussies announced that Martin Visser, a "new Australian" who had been a top small boat sailor in Holland before emigrating Down Under, would handle the start and then turn the helm back to Hardy. *Gretel*'s twin wheels made this especially easy. Visser, a bulldog of a man obviously endowed with some qualities associated with the Dutch, made the switch look good by taking the start with a neatly executed safe leeward at the buoy end, and, with Hardy back in charge, *Gretel* became the first challenger since 1934 to lead at the first mark. Excitement rippled through the spectator fleet and built higher when *Intrepid* swept into the lead on the spinnaker reach. The tension was increased even more by gradually deteriorating visibility, which had been a mile at the start. By the time the boats moved onto the second windward leg after completing the first triangle of the race, they had disappeared in a gray, woolly void.

Only the inner screen of escort vessels could see them, and just barely, as they engaged in a multi-tack duel in the gathering gloom, with *Gretel* inching closer on every flip-flop. Finally, with conditions virtually down to zero visibility, the race committee pulled another first—they called the race. Fortunately, as to possible reactions to the decision, *Intrepid* was still in control, but it was obvious that *Gretel* was capable of giving a battle and the Americans had a real fight on their hands.

After still another layday, this potential became a reality in the first Cup race ever run on a Sunday. Before a swarming fleet of over 1,000 spectator craft, biggest since 1962, the Twelves got off to a start just before the deadline for cancellation, as a light southwester riffled in over the sunny seascape to save the day, but not before two more weird "firsts." On the way out to the start, Van Dyck, a vital member of the *Intrepid* team, picked up a can of orange soda for a sip and was stung by a bee that had settled on it. He suffered a violent reaction and serious swelling, and, before the amazed eyes of the milling spectators, was airlifted by helicopter to Newport Naval Hospital for treatment. The spectators, shaken by this sudden crisis, were further rocked when a supposed mine was spotted in among the boats, but this bit of drama became comic opera when it was finally identified as a fish-net float.

Finally, just in time to initiate signals for the starting procedure, the gentle breeze set the stage for perhaps the most highly publicized yachting incident since *America*'s 1851 adventure. Visser was at the wheel again as the boats circled slowly and warily near the windward end of the line. All the maneuvering led to a situation in which *Intrepid* started down from a windward position, close reaching at a good clip for the committee boat's stern, as the 30-seconds-to-go signal dropped. *Gretel* had been idly luffing up from a bit ahead and down to leeward with very little way on, with Visser obviously hoping to catch Ficker "barging." Under the rules, a boat to leeward of another in the approach to the starting line is under no obligation to give a windward boat room at the starting mark, and, if the opening at the stern of the committee boat could be sealed off before the starting gun was fired, *Intrepid* would be burdened with this barging role and would have to bear off under *Gretel* or round up on the wrong side of the committee boat.

Visser seemed to have Ficker dead to rights except for one oversight. *Gretel* wasn't going fast enough to get to the opening and close it off before the gun. It has been surmised in some quarters that Hardy, who was supposed to trim the main sheet while Visser was on the helm, couldn't stop acting like a skipper and was so fascinated by the developing situation that he failed to trim, and therefore *Gretel* did not have enough speed to accomplish the maneuver, but this is all conjecture.

In any event, the gun went off with both boats short of the line, and at the sound of the gun, a new Rule, 42.1(e), came into effect as the only one to apply. Under it, *Gretel* could no longer sail above close-hauled, but the prospect of really getting *Intrepid* in trouble had gripped the Aussies so completely, that Visser continued to luff up as though he still had rights to do so, with the crew yelling "Up, Up, UP!" (a call for rights from the leeward boat) until *Gretel*'s bow raked along *Intrepid*'s side just aft of the mast approximately 14 seconds after the gun and the time when Visser was supposed to have borne off to no higher than close-hauled. Ironically, had Visser done the latter, he would no doubt have had a good safe leeward, and *Gretel* would probably have held the lead for the whole race. The light breeze was just to her liking—her very best conditions against *Intrepid*, heavier, with less acceleration out of tacks in light stuff.

Winning the third race

Very few spectators knew that there had been contact or that both boats had protested. The fleet, a great cross-section of what the sport of yachting had become in the 1970s, with few yachts over 100 feet, many small cabin cruisers and auxiliaries, and even open outboards, was too far away to see the little pieces of red cloth in the rigging of each boat, and the excitement of the moment was in seeing a great race develop.

Gretel, recovering from the bounce off *Intrepid* at the start that had deposited her bow fitting on the American's deck and given Ficker a good lead to work with, gradually closed up in a tacking duel, but Ficker had managed to stay ahead under the constant threat of the ever-surging *Gretel* until they started the fifth leg, a dead run in gradually fading air. Then, with her rig slacked forward noticeably to keep her sails as full as possible and with crewman Dave Forbes handling the wheel, *Gretel* got the best of a downwind jibing duel and slid in the lead halfway down the leg. Pandemonium echoed around the spectator fleet as wild Aussie cheers rang across the calm water, and they continued right through the final leg as Hardy kept *Gretel* ahead by a margin of 1:07. Rockets arched through the evening sky, but the situation soon fizzled to bitter controversy when the protest became known.

The New York Yacht Club Race Committee had no choice but to disqualify *Gretel*, with Chairman Devereux Barker announcing the decision in measured tones the next day to a hushed press conference that immediately erupted into a donnybrook of excited questions, heated denials by Visser that he agreed with the findings, and the beginnings of a full-fledged international incident. People with no knowledge of the sailing rules pontificated on the subject, and the controversy reached far into non-nautical surroundings, but the fact remained that one boat must be disqualified when there is a collision, and the infamously famous 42.1(e) of the International Yacht Racing Rules put *Gretel* unmistakably in the wrong. Had there been a neutral protest committee to come to the inevitable decision, rather than the beleaguered New York Yacht Club committee having to act as prosecutor, judge and jury, some of the hysterical brouhaha could have been avoided.

And so the score stood 2-0 for *Intrepid* rather than 1-1, and the Aussies went about the remaining races in an atmosphere of bitter defeatism. The celebrated foul will live long as the most memorable incident in *Intrepid*'s career, although the job she and her crew did in the following races was a great one that preserved her special ranking among the legendary yachts.

The third race was almost devoid of fireworks, a letdown from the high excitement of the first week, but Ficker forged a workman-like victory by taking the start and holding onto the lead with a flawless race. In a fresh, sunny southwester that built from 10 to 18 knots, he controlled Visser completely in the pre-start maneuvers, gaining a leeward spot on starboard tack that enabled him to force *Gretel* over the starting line just before gun. The only way that Visser could get back to the line was to tack away on port and dip the line, giving away distance to leeward all the while. Ficker dipped back to the favored buoy end on starboard and flipped over on port tack to cover *Gretel* with an instant advantage that translated to a minute lead at the first mark. *Gretel*'s main chance to break through came on the dead run again, but this time Van Dyck, back on board, called the jibing angles precisely right, while *Gretel* took a flyer that only wasted distance, standing away on the opposite jibe while *Intrepid* aimed straight for the mark at maximum speed.

In the fourth race, in a moderate easterly and with the spectator fleet dwindling, Ficker seemed to have the Cup safely tucked away with another 4-0 sweep as he managed an almost carbon copy of the third race start and then held his lead by the unorthodox tactic of failing to cover *Gretel* on the windward legs. Knowing her faster acceleration in this wind strength, he preferred to avoid a tacking duel with her and instead sailed *Intrepid* strictly on boat speed and on playing lifts and headers regardless of Hardy's moves. It worked for five legs, and he entered the home stretch with a lead of 1:02 that looked absolutely safe.

This time however, going against the book backfired. Halfway up the leg, with *Intrepid* sagging down on *Gretel*'s leeward bow after at first seeming able to fetch the finish, *Gretel* suddenly found a fresh lift and surged high up on *Intrepid*'s windward quarter. Too late,

A happy crew relaxes and congratulates Bill Ficker after final victory

Intrepid came back on port tack through an increasingly bad header to cover, found she couldn't cross the challenger, and had to tack under *Gretel*'s lee bow.

Routine expectation of the finish of the series turned to stunned consternation in the boats around the finish line as the two Twelves came closer in the dying air. Once more *Intrepid* tried to tack over, and this time she had to cross under *Gretel*'s stern. Hardy kept good speed on *Gretel*, gauged one short hitch just right at the finishing buoy, and put her across the line about 60 yards ahead of *Intrepid*, now so badly slowed by the dying air that she took 1:02 to wallow through those last agonizing yards. One of the most amazing comebacks in sailing history had kept the series alive in an unbelievable reprieve of Aussie hopes, and there were many might-have-beens over what course events could have taken if the score had been 2-2 instead of 3-1 at this point.

A layday, a weather cancellation and another layday put the fifth race over until Monday, September 28, the longest run of any America's Cup series, and Ficker and his flawlessly operating crew kept *Intrepid*'s niche in history safe by taking one of the closest match races of all time. It was a gray, autumnal day, with a light, shifty northerly off the mainland, and Hardy, taking over starting duties again, gained the advantage in the windward berth at the committee boat end to put the pressure on right away.

In the first series of tacks, however, his slight hesitation at two junctures as *Intrepid* tacked away finally put *Gretel* on *Intrepid*'s leeward bow just as a shifting, fresher puff hit the defender. It was enough of a lift to put *Intrepid* up on *Gretel*'s beam and in control, and in a long, tense struggle, Ficker never let that control lapse. Trying to move out by applying a loose cover, he twice had to come back to a smotheringly tight blanket to hold the slippery *Gretel*, and he made several split-second tactical moves that cemented the advantage. After carrying *Gretel* beyond the lay line on the second windward leg when leading by only a length or two, Ficker tacked away smoothly while *Gretel* carried on, wasting distance, and the fifth downwind jibing duel, an agonizing affair that took a full hour, was faultlessly executed to keep *Gretel* off *Intrepid*'s wind.

At the last mark, *Intrepid's* crew made its final contribution of perfect execution, allowing Ficker to tack immediately around the buoy onto a slant that could fetch the finish, while Hardy had to waste precious seconds sailing away from the mark while his crew cleared gear from the spinnaker-to-genoa change.

Hardy wriggled up the last leg like a desperate fish trying to get off the hook, making unnecessary tacks in an attempt to lure *Intrepid* into a repeat of the fourth race mistake, but Ficker would have none of it this time. The lead that had been 20 seconds after the fifth leg was stretched to 1:44 and the Cup was secure once more.

Although a superboat had been virtually turned into an underdog by the march of events, she was still a champion and a winner when it counted most. Artistically, this should perhaps have been the end of her career, but her story went on to mesh with, and be an important part of, that of her successor, *Courageous.*

289
Intrepid

Proudly sporting "Ficker is quicker" banner, *Intrepid* returns to Newport, R.I., on last tow in after winning fifth race

18

Courageous

Intrepid's story would seem hard to match, but *Courageous* managed to create some legends of her own, a bit different in emphasis but equally as dramatic, in the next two America's Cup campaigns. For the record books, she joined the old *Columbia* of the turn of the century and *Intrepid* as a two-time winner, but her victories in the actual Cup matches were not all that exciting. It was in her hard-fought campaigns to gain the defender's berth that the fireworks were produced, and *Intrepid* played a major role in sparking them.

Courageous was a lineal descendant of *Intrepid*. Many of her syndicate members had been with the older boat in 1967 and 1970, and she was also from the design board of Olin Stephens. Turning away from the relatively radical experimentation that had produced the unsuccessful *Valiant* in 1970, the first time a new boat of his design had failed to win the defense trials in her maiden year, Stephens had gone back to his earlier line of thinking for *Courageous*. She embodied new ideas, but she was descended from the *Vim-Columbia-Constellation-Intrepid* series much more than from the full-bodied, heavy *Valiant*.

Valiant and the Chance-modified *Intrepid* in 1970 had proved sluggish, with steering problems and poor acceleration out of tacks and maneuvers, so *Courageous* was lighter and shorter on the waterline with more sail area. Her rudder was well aft and bigger than in immediate predecessors, with a trim tab, and she had a thinner keel and garboard sections. This was intended to make her livelier, more maneuverable, quicker to accelerate and fast in light air, but the shorter waterline, which was a measurement benefit but theoretically limited the top potential of her hull speed, was compensated for by long, low overhangs. When there was enough breeze to heel her, and a longer waterline would therefore be helpful, her entire after overhang would be in the water, and most of the one at the bow, adding greatly to her effective waterline length. She was 66' x 45'6" x 12' x 8'10" and carried 1770 feet of sail.

Her connection with *Intrepid* was even further emphasized when Bill Ficker was nominated as her skipper in the summer of 1973, and construction was begun at the Minneford Yard on New York's City Island, where *Intrepid* had been built. She and the other new boat for 1974, *Mariner*, were the first to be built of aluminum, now possible through a change in the scantling specifications of Lloyds of London under which 12-Meters must be constructed.

Before she was barely a set of frames behind barred doors, she ran into the first of many obstacles that she always seemed to be overcoming for the rest of her career. The oil embargo and the sense of crisis generated by it in the fall of 1973 scared off some contributors to the syndicate, which was the last, incidentally, to be completely privately financed without benefit of tax deductions. All others since then have been sponsored by public groups or service academy foundations that qualified for tax exemptions.

Construction was halted for a while and her career looked like a short one indeed. During this period of uncertainty, Ficker had to give a definite answer to another commitment for the summer of 1974, a business one not related to the America's Cup, and he reluctantly backed out of the *Courageous* project. A few weeks later, the green light came on again for *Courageous*, and the syndicate turned to Bob Bavier, who had salvaged *Constellation*'s weak-starting campaign in 1964 and then swamped *Sovereign* in a 4-0 runaway.

The early book was that the main competition for *Courageous* would come from *Mariner*. Ted Turner, the controversial Georgian

A bow-to-bow approach to a start, with both boats luffing, typical of the
Intrepid—Courageous in-fighting in the 1974 trials

with a fine racing record in everything from dinghies to *American Eagle*, the 12-Meter converted to ocean racing, was to be *Mariner's* skipper. A fierce competitor with a will to win matched only by the stentorian quality of his voice, Turner looked like a natural, and Chance was thought by many to be the logical contender for Olin Stephens' role as top dog in 12-Meter designers. Some believed his claims that he had made *Intrepid* faster in 1970 with his modifications to her design, though there was a school of thought that strongly disagreed, and he had also had experience working with the French Twelves. The scuttle was that chance had come up with a "breakthrough" this time, if you believed rumors seeping out of the Stevens Institute in Hoboken, N.J. where the designs were tank tested.

The doubters were shown to be all too right the first time *Mariner* and *Courageous* raced, however. Chance had produced an odd after-end configuration with two flat, cut off "transoms" under water, a great, bulbous after section, a deep blade rudder and a small keel well forward. Knowledgeable observers were overheard at her launching saying things like "If he's right, everything I know about boat design is wrong," and there was considerable interest when the boats met for the first time in the New York Yacht Club Annual Regatta on Long Island Sound June 1-2. *Valiant*, with the veteran George Hinman at the helm and slated to be *Mariner's* trail horse, was an added starter but had not been tuned to racing condition. The suspense soon vanished, as *Courageous* won by 3:50 the first day and the whopping margin of 7:57 the second, with *Valiant* third both times, and the writing was all too clearly on the wall for *Mariner*. Despite a complete re-design and reconstruction of her after end, possible in an aluminum boat, and the replacement of Turner with Dennis Conner, *Mariner* never became a serious contender. It was the last of her, but not of Turner, in the *Courageous* story.

The failure of *Mariner* in such a definite way so early on seemed to make *Courageous* an overwhelming favorite, but there was one other element in the picture that no one had much considered. *Intrepid* was coming back. She had been written off by many when the change to aluminum was authorized, as it was generally believed that wooden boats could not remain competitive against the new metal ones.

Intrepid had been bought by a West Coast syndicate that intended to campaign her under private financing but ran into difficulties and eventually turned her over to an organization called the Seattle Sailing Foundation. This had been set up to promote sailing and sailing instruction in the Pacific Northwest, supported by deductible donations, and, with an experienced Six-Meter sailor named Sunny Vynne in charge, management of *Intrepid* was assumed. A public campaign to raise funds, with any size donation accepted, met with enthusiastic response, and, with the combination of her now being a "people's boat," a wooden one with a great record already established, and from a new area in the long history of the America's Cup, *Intrepid* became the sentimental favorite of press and public. Gerry Driscoll, a thoroughly experienced Southern California racing sailor and boat builder, was her skipper.

Competitively, she soon established herself as more than a sentimental contender. She had four months of training on the West Coast and was then trucked east in time for the first trials of the campaign, the Preliminary Series, off Newport, R.I. June 24-29. *Courageous* beat her by small margins in their first pairing in light air, but *Intrepid* came back in stronger air the next day they were paired and took two convincing wins. Bavier and Driscoll had been together on *Constellation* for a short while in 1964, had great respect for each other, and were obviously in for a hot summer of battling it out.

With *Mariner*'s demise an early certainty, all interest focused on the *Intrepid-Courageous* confrontation, and it sustained a long summer of drama and excitement. Driscoll had been convinced that *Intrepid '67* was a lot faster than *Intrepid '70*, and she had been lightened considerably and returned to her original configuration. Young John Marshall of the North sail loft had made some innovative two-ply main sails for her, and the four months of practice in the Pacific had given her crew a sharp edge. They were young West Coast deck-ape types who had been welded into a smooth group under Andy McGowan, an experienced 12-Meter and ocean racing sailor from New York.

In the July trials, Bavier and Driscoll staged hammer-and-tongs starts with the closest kind of in-fighting, and the two boats slugged it out around the course with *Intrepid* ending up ahead by a 4-2 margin. *Intrepid* was operating smoothly with few gear failures, while *Courageous* was plagued with gear problems and troubles with her mainsail, which was made of the new synthetic called Kevlar. The sail was tremendously strong in direct tension, but tended to break down under flexing, such as when a sail luffs, and eventually had to be discarded. It had been thought of as the greatest invention since Jello for a while.

When *Intrepid* took both of the special races held for the Twelves on the first and last days of the New York Yacht Club cruise, the first in light air by 1:12 after several changes of lead, and the second by holding onto an 18-second lead throughout a race sailed in a 25 knot gear-buster, the stage was set for the final trials in August, and *Courageous* had definitely become the underdog. Signs reading "Knock on Wood" appeared all over Newport, and the popular appeal of *Intrepid* continued to grow. The general public seemed to delight in the "Establishment" boat, *Courageous*, losing out to the wooden "People's Boat." Tension was high in the *Courageous* camp, transmitting itself to the supposedly gracious living her crew and syndicate were enjoying at Hammersmith Farm, the Auchincloss estate on the rocky shore of Narragansett Bay where Jackie Kennedy had summered as a girl.

The *Courageous* group concentrated on boat speed while getting ready for the August trials and even ordered some North sails, departing from her inventory of all Hood sails. Paradoxically, Ted Hood, who had made these sails, was invited aboard as alternate helmsman and tactician.

Intrepid opened the August skirmishing with a 31-second victory, helped by a spinnaker foul-up on *Courageous*, but Bavier got the new boat back on top with four straight wins. The first was a real squeaker by two seconds, and the next three were 1:31, 4:51, and ten seconds. There were those who thought this was enough for the New York Yacht Club Cup Committee to select *Courageous*, but the margins were so close that the series was continued, and *Intrepid* made a magnificent comeback with three straight wins. The tension had become almost unbearable, and the atmosphere in the *Courageous* camp

Southern Cross (KA4) port tacks *Courageous* just before the second race start in 1974, forcing the latter to tack away, but the International Jury on the powerboat next to *Courageous* said it wasn't a foul

was jittery at best as the series ran on to the last possible date. The rules said a defender had to be picked by September 2nd, and here the boats were at 4-4, with that date coming up. *Courageous* had suffered from a few errors in the last three races, and there were rumors that the crew was unhappy with the afterguard, but it wasn't until an hour before the boats were to tow out for the last start, with the crews assembling on the piers at Newport Shipyard, that syndicate manager Bob McCullough approached Bavier, who was already aboard and making preparations to leave port.

McCullough called him aside and without preamble said, "Bob, you're not going to sail today. Ted Hood's taking over."

News of this bombshell spread through the fleet as the boats towed out to the start on a day of blustery southwest wind, and everyone knew that the winner of this race would be the defender. Hood had ordered Hood sails to be used, and, with Halsey Harrishoff navigating, he sailed *Courageous* superbly to a 1:47 victory, while *Intrepid* lost what chance she might have had with a temporary backstay failure that momentarily prevented her from tacking when she wanted to.

And so the gallant wooden boat ended her competitive career. After a change of ownership, Driscoll regained control of her in 1977 but was unable to arrange backing for her for another try at the defense, and she was eventually sold to Baron Bich, the French industrialist who has gathered a total of seven Twelve Meters under his wing in his unsuccessful attempts to mount a challenge.

With *Intrepid* finally out of her way, *Courageous* went on to as much glory as the older wooden boat had enjoyed. Her competition in the 1974 America's Cup match was the Australian boat *Southern Cross*, designed by Bob Miller and sailed by Jim Hardy, who had been *Gretel II*'s skipper in 1970. She was the first challenger from Western Australia, and her owner was Alan Bond, a brash real estate promoter from that remote area. Bond, who exuded cocky confidence in every word and action, evidently felt that bravado was the best ploy with which to carry off a challenge, and he had most of his homeland and many Americans convinced that this was going to be the most serious challenge yet, with an odds-on chance to lift the Cup for the first time in 104 years of challenges. He also made a great deal of noise about how the New York Yacht Club was going to bend the rules in its own favor and make Southern Cross' task all that much more difficult.

It was a great letdown, therefore, when all this bombast produced one of the most one-sided losing efforts to date, and Hood sailed *Courageous* to four easy wins by margins of 4:54, 1:11, 5:27 and 7:19. It was a series devoid of drama and significant incident, and it left *Courageous* at a pinnacle of success as the ultimate in 12-Meter development.

As with *Columbia*, *Constellation* and *Intrepid* ('67) before her, all convincing winners in 4-0 sweeps, there was conjecture that *Courageous* now represented the ultimate and that it would be very hard to surpass her with new designs. Everyone admitted that the variations possible on a 12-Meter under the rules had been narrowed down to very small tolerances. Boats on which something a bit different had been tried, like *Mariner*, or *Southern Cross*, with her greater length and wetted surface, had not proved out, and sailmakers were saying that differences in sails were now probably more important than small refinements in 12-Meter design.

And yet there was no dearth of people willing to prove otherwise for the 1977 campaign, the next year in which one would be possible under New York Yacht Club's policy of no less than three years between challenges. The challenge fever was higher than ever, with an interesting new note added by Sweden's entry into the lists. Baron Bich would be back again for France, and the Aussies were putting two boats in, Alan Bond with a new boat, and a re-vamped *Gretel II* sponsored by Royal Sydney Yacht Squadron.

Olin Stephens was asked to design a new boat, and Ted Hood also went to the boards to produce his own design. He had had previous experience with *Nefertiti*, which he had designed and sailed in 1962, losing to Bus Mosbacher in *Weatherly* in the trials. Both *Enterprise*, the Stephens design, and Hood's *Independence*, would be sponsored by service academy foundations for tax purposes, *Enterprise* by the N.Y. State Maritime College at Fort Schulyer, and the *Independence* by the Merchant Marine Academy at Kings Point, which had been *Mariner's* sponsor. And how would *Courageous* fit into all this?

Although there was general acknowledgment that it would be hard to improve on her basic design, there was the feeling that new boats could perhaps do a bit better, and she was acquired by Hood's group as what might be called a glorified trial horse. *Independence* would clearly be number one in the camp, but *Courageous* would be given every chance to prove herself as a valid contender. Lee Loomis, a veteran Long Island yachtsman, was to be manager of the syndicate and it was his idea to have *Courageous* as well sailed as possible, albeit as the second-stringer in the stable. So who was to be her skipper?

Enter Ted Turner, the discredited skipper of *Mariner* who had been eased out of the 1974 campaign as a supposed failure. This had rankled the proud Georgian, who felt that he had had no chance at all to prove himself with *Mariner*, and who had been burning up ocean racing courses as usual in the interim. He had also made a name for himself as a national sports figure by buying the Atlanta Braves baseball and Atlanta Hawks basketball franchises and immediately becoming embroiled up to his ever-present cigar in controversy. Baseball Commissioner Bowie Kuhn had suspended him for improper action in connection with a free agent player (mainly for shooting off the famous Turner "Mouth of the South" at an unauthorized time), and he had made headlines by suspending his manager and taking over in the dugout during a losing streak.

He had also managed to win the Congressional Cup, a match race round-robin series in Long Beach, California that had always before been won by Californians, had done well on the Southern Circuit, and was itching to prove himself in the America's Cup arena. He had not been invited to take part in practice sails between *Independence* and *Courageous* in the fall of 1976, but the old boat was turned over to him in the spring of 1977 and he was given a free hand in selecting his crew and getting her ready for the competition, while Hood concentrated on his new boat.

Enterprise was to be sailed by Lowell North, the West Coast sailmaker with a long list of successes, including the Star world championship and Olympic medals, and Hood's major rival in the sailmaking field. An interesting summer of competition between the two

About the only times *Courageous* and *Australia* were close was before the starts

Courageous (left) had *Southern Cross* safely tucked away early in most of the 1974 races

Enterprise (US27) is about to pass *Courageous* after rounding first mark of last race of 1977 July trials, but *Courageous* took over on the last leg again in a crucial race

new boats was envisioned, with Turner as a sort of odd man out.

Turner immediately became involved in controversy when North refused to make sails for him, and much was made of it in the press, with Turner styling himself as the last amateur yachtsman battling the professionals. This also served to heighten interest in the North-Turner encounters as well as the North-Hood encounters. Turner's sails were the province of young Robby Doyle of the Hood loft, who cut them himself and was in charge of their trim while racing, and it turned out that they served Turner well. Another young sailor chosen by Turner for his crew was Gary Jobson, whose experience had been almost entirely in small one designs, and he became an extremely important member of the *Courageous* team as tactician.

Not only was Turner in controversies nautically, he also managed to get into trouble socially in Newport with unguarded remarks and actions at parties ashore. With a voice of a peculiar timbre that carries his southern accent across the noisiest room like a foghorn cutting through mist, he can pass a private aside to a nearby companion that just happens to carry to everyone else in the room, and anything injudicious he happens to say becomes public property immediately.

All the factors of the Turner image combined to make a lively press, and the 1977 America's Cup campaign was by far the most widely covered in history, largely due to his reputation and individualistic charisma. Before the summer was over he had become a form of folk hero, with crowds following him down Thames Street in Newport whenever he ventured off the boat, thrusting autograph papers at him, shaking his hand and waving and yelling. Pretty girls would run up to kiss him, squealing in delight, and Turner, a handsome, imposing figure with head well above the crowd, would brandish his cigar and let out his standard cry of "aw—RIIIGHT!" at the top of his lungs.

On the water, there was no nonsense, however. *Courageous* was well-organized and well-sailed, and she made few mistakes. Those with behind-the-scenes information realized that her hull form was still competitive, since most of the new boats were spinoffs from her. Stephens had made a few modifications in developing *Enterprise*, but she was not all that different, and Hood had had the *Courageous* plans while he was working on *Independence*. Also, Johan Valentijn, co-designer of Bond's challenger *Australia*, had been working at Sparkman & Stephens when *Courageous* was designed. His partner was *Southern Cross'* designer Bob Miller, who, for reasons known only to himself, had changed his name to Ben Lexcen.

When the Preliminary Trials started off Newport June 18th, Turner had his crew tuned and ready, and he came to win races, while the two new boats were more concerned with testing sails and gear and developing boat speed. In the underdog role, Turner felt that *Courageous* had to win and keep winning, and he set out to do just that convincingly. His record was 10-1, losing once to *Enterprise* by seven seconds, and once squeaking by the same boat by a mere two feet, and, despite all the excuses made in the other camps, *Courageous* had shaken off the underdog tag when these trials concluded. They were only "Preliminary"—a form of shakedown in a way, but *Courageous* could not be ignored any more. She had become the boat to beat.

She almost went back to the underdog role in the July trials. The new boats began to shake out wrinkles and concentrate more on tactics, and it was also evident that the sails on *Courageous*, which had not been replaced, were getting a bit tired. For a while the series produced a round-robin standoff, as *Independence* was beating *Enterprise*, *Enterprise* was now taking *Courageous*, and *Courageous* consistently beating *Independence*. Then *Enterprise* began to put it all together, and she turned the tables twice on *Independence* in their last meetings, and had taken four in a row from *Courageous*.

The last pairing of the July series on July 27th was *Enterprise-Courageous* on a crystal-clear day of gentle southwest breeze and smooth sea, and there was a special electricity in the air as the boats prepared for their start. To most of the experts, it appeared that *Enterprise* was finally on her way, and that this was the last stand for Turner and the *Courageous* crew. It was a close race from an even start, with the lead changing hands twice, but *Enterprise* came from close astern on the first reaching leg, blanketed *Courageous* to take the lead, and fought her off in a luffing duel further down the leg. As they rounded the leeward mark for the last windward leg, *Enterprise* had a comfortable half-minute lead, and many in the spectator fleet,

Ted Turner in, uncharacteristically, repose

figuring it was all over, headed for port instead of following the last leg. They missed a good one, and what proved to be one of the crucial moments of the summer.

Enterprise was sporting her dark green genoa known as the "garbage bag" because of its color and shiny texture, while *Courageous* had at last gotten some new sails and was using a new five-oz. Hood genoa. The breeze picked up a bit from about 8 to 11 knots, perhaps a touch too much for the garbage bag, and Turner, ever the fighter, began a tacking duel. North covered for several tacks, as *Courageous*, with Jobson picking lifts and headers just right as was his wont all summer, gradually gained. A third of the way up the leg, *Enterprise*, on starboard tack, crossed ahead, but was now close enough for the shadow of her sails to flick across *Courageous* in the passing.

The obvious move would have been a quick flip to cover, or perhaps even a lee bow tack, but, to the consternation of everyone watching, *Enterprise* stood on the eastward for 15 minutes without tacking, allowing *Courageous* to go uncovered toward the west, where the afternoon lifts always come from in a Newport southwester. When the boats finally converged, *Courageous* had a five length lead, and Turner held it by covering carefully the rest of the way in to win by 43 seconds.

This one leg seemed to turn the whole picture around. When the Final Trials began August 16th, *Courageous* quickly moved on top again. *Independence*, despite new sails, had not gained boat speed, and *Enterprise* seemed to be in a state of panic, making tactical mistakes and still experimenting with sails. Fortified with more new sails, Turner sailed with increasing confidence and won going away with a 10-1 record (the only loss was to *Independence*). On August 30th, *Enterprise* (which had changed skipper and tactician in a last desperate move) was defeated once more, and the America's Cup committee came alongside the berth where the *Courageous* crew was waiting hopefully after their return to port and gave the expected news that *Courageous* would once again be the defender.

And so she joined *Intrepid*, which she had barely beaten in 1974, as a two-time defender, but here the script deviated. Where the wooden boat had had so much trouble staving off the potentially faster *Gretel II* in 1970, *Courageous* outclassed *Australia* which had beaten the French and Swedes as definitely as she had *Southern Cross*. The consensus was that the hulls were approximately even, with perhaps still an edge to *Courageous*, but Robbie Doyle's headsails (and their trim), the slick work of the crew, Jobson's tactics, and Turner's cool competence and concentration combined to make a runaway.

A symbol of the supremacy of the American crew was in the way they managed headsail changes. These were done so smoothly that they often went undetected by all but the keenest observers, while the Aussie changes were highly noticeable for their lack of coordination. All Turner needed was clear air, and he usually preferred a spot off the leeward bow of the challenger at the start of the races, so that he could gradually squeeze the other boat up and feed her bad air

A happy *Courageous* crew, with Turner smiling broadly, enters Newport harbor in triumph after final 1977 victory

until she had to tack away. This was the pattern in every race, and Courageous was never behind on a crossing tack or at a mark in a series that ran the gamut of air from light to moderate, but never heavy. With Turner sailing steadily and conservatively once he had his lead, the margins were 1:40, 1:03, 2:32 and 2:25.

The biggest excitement of the series came after it was all over in the wild reception *Courageous* received when her tow brought her back into Newport for the last time in the slanting, hazy sunlight of a late September afternoon. The harbor and shoreline were jammed beyond belief with boats and people. Bands were playing, sirens screaming, tons of Freon were blasting into the misty atmosphere, and fire hoses sprayed up in the pale rays of the sun, as her champagne swilling crew brought her alongside in their final hour of triumph. Turner was the center of it, waving laughing and pouring down the liquid as his relaxed crew celebrated around him, as well they might. They had sailed a legendary yacht to her finest hours over every conceivable obstacle.

Index

Adams, Charles Francis, 144, 145
Adams, John Quincy, 21
Adriana, 199
Alden, John, 185, 231
Alfonso, King, 196, 197
Aloha, 113–125, 230
Alva, 47, 49, 55–56, 89
America, 18, 27, 29–45, 162, 166, 215, 230, 258, 283
American Eagle, 260, 263, 264, 265, 294
Angelita, 132
Anglesey, Marquis of, 36
Antarna, 128
Ara, 47, 59–62, 101
Arrow, 41
Aspinwall, William H., 6
Assheton-Smith, Thomas, 2, 5
Astor, John Jacob, 48, 101
Astor, Vincent, 101
Astor, William, 7
Astor family, 13, 47, 89, 152
Atalanta, 7, 68
Athenia, 100
Atlantic, 49, 137–149, 155, 193, 194, 196, 212
Aurora, 39, 41–42
Australia, 303, 305

Bahama Star, 226
Barker, Devereux, 287
Barr, Captain Charles, 139, 140
Bartram, Burr, 260
Baruna, 185
Bavier, Bob, 263, 292, 295, 296, 298
Beavor-Webb, John, 71, 72, 75

Becket, John, 20
Bennett, James Gordon, 13, 90
Bertram, Dick, 237
Bich, Baron Marcel, 274, 278, 298
Bliss, Zenas, 166
Bolero, 185, 238
Bond, Alan, 299
Brassey, Sir Thomas, 5–6, 114
Bright, Ward, 146–147
Brilliant, 42
Brittain, William, 222
Brown, M. Bayard, 90
Brown, Nicholas, 90
Brown, Captain Richard, 33, 34, 42
Brown, William H., 31
Burgess, W. Starling, 162, 164, 194

Cadwaladar, Emily Roebling, 151–152
Cambria, 44
Camilla, 44
Carib, 231
Caribbee, 231, 232
Carlisle, Allan P., 216–217
Carstens, Willie, 203
Chanticleer, 245–255
Chance, Britton, Jr., 274–277, 291
Chancegger, 273, 277
Charles II, King, 1
Chisholm, Hugh, 175
Christina, 128, 175
Cleopatra, Queen, 1, 18
Cleopatra's Barge, 5, 17–27, 245
Cleveland, Grover, 69
Colonna, Jerry, 248

Columbia, 65, 260, 264, 265, 273, 276, 277, 291
Conner, Dennis, 294
Connie, 263, 265, 273, 276
Constellation, 260, 263, 264, 273
Constitution, 271
Conte di Savoia, 154
Coronet, 114
Corsair I, 7, 14, 67–68, 89
Corsair II, 68–71, 89
Corsair III, 71–83, 89, 152
Corsair IV, 77, 83–84, 89, 100, 175, 176
Courageous, 291–306
Cramer, Corwith, Jr., 237
Cramp, William, 7
Crane, Clinton H., 11–13, 56, 59, 71
Crawford, Earl of, 139
Crowninshield, Mr. and Mrs. Benjamin, 21
Crowninshield, Benjamin, Jr., 24, 26
Crowninshield, George, 5, 17–27
Curtis, Cyrus H. K., 94–97

Dalzell, Briggs, 274
Dame Pattie, 263, 264, 268
Danginn, 175
Darrell, Bert, 199
Dauntless, 141
Davidson, Kenneth, 162–163
Davies, Joseph E., 132
Decatur, Stephen, Jr., 272
Detroit, 196, 197
Dickson, Bob, 227
Diver, 30
Djinn, 84–86
Dodge, Horace E., 94
Dorade, 162
Drexel, Anthony J., 89–90
Driscoll, Gerry, 295
Dubuque, 80

Edlu, 162
Edward VII, King, 41, 142
Egger, Herman, 273
Electra, 6–7
Elena, 144, 145, 194, 215
Elizabeth I, Queen, 1
Elizabeth (cutter), 2
Endeavour I, 62, 164, 166–171
Endeavour II, 84, 168–171
Enterprise, 62, 162, 164, 271
Enterprise (12-meter), 299–305
Escapade, 216
Eventide, 184
Evinrude, Ralph, 246–255

Fales, DeCoursey, 193, 200, 203, 204–207
Ferris, Theodore, 101
Ficker, Bill, 276, 280, 283, 285, 286, 288, 289
Finisterre, 229–243
Fire-Fly, 6

Fleischman, Max, 98
Fleur de Lys, 139
Flying Cloud, 90
Forbes, Dave, 286
Forstmann, Julius, 152
Foto, 237
France, 278
Freak, 39, 41
Freeman, Ned, 237
Furor, 71

Gabor, Zsa Zsa, 132
Galatea, 71
Gardner, William, 138
Genesta, 71
George IV, King, 1, 2
Gerry, E. T., 6, 13
Gibbs, W. E., 152
Gimcrack, 29, 30
Gipsey Queen, 39
Gloucester, 71
Gonzolus, ChiChi, 252
Gould, Jay, 7, 13, 68, 94
Gretel, 277–289
Gretel II, 298, 299
Guinevere, 145

Haida, 98
Hamilton, James, 33
Hammond, James, 97–98
Hammond, Paul, 194, 198–199
Hardy, Jim, 277, 280, 288
Heaton, Peter, 2
Heritage, 277, 278
Herreshoff, L. Francis, 210, 215, 227
Hertz, John, Jr., 217, 222
Hinman, George, 278, 294
Hohenzollern, 138
Hood, Ted, 264, 274
Hood, Warwick, 263, 271
Hope, Bob, 252
Hoyt, Sherman, 164, 198
Hoyt, Mrs. W. S., 59
Hussar I, 129–131
Hussar II, 131
Hutton, Mrs. Marjorie Post, 129–132
Hughes, Howard, 98–100

Independence, 299, 300, 303, 305
Intrepid (yacht), 257–300
Intrepid (frigate), 271–273

Jaffray, Edward S., 6
James, Arthur Curtiss, 114–125
Jefferson, 18, 27
Johnson, Robert, 222–223
Jolie Brise, 199
Jones, John Paul, 164
Julyan, Herbert E., 98

Kamehameha II, King, 27
Kittenger, Commander Theodore A., 76
Knapp, Arthur, 166
Kurrewa, 274

Lambert, Gerald, 144, 145–146
Langford, Frances (Mrs. Ralph Evinrude), 246, 248, 252
Laverock, 34–36
Leeds, William B., 55
Leopold, King, 2
Liberty, 90
Lipton, Sir Thomas, 14, 62, 138
Loomis, Alfred, 138
Lorillard, Jacob, 6
Louis Philippe, King, 2
Lounger IV, 97–98
Ludwig, Daniel, 175
Lysistrata, 90
Lyndonia, 94–97

McCullough, Bob, 273, 276–277
MacDonald, Joseph, 77
McKinley, William, 69
Madison, James, 21
Magic, 215
Malabars, 185
Margarita, 89–90
Maria, 30
Mariner, 292, 294, 295, 299, 300, 301
Marshall, Wilson, 138
Mary, 1
Mary Taylor, 33
Mastico, 272
Mellon, Dr. Matthew T., 217
Memphis, 44
Meteor, 138
Mitchell, Carleton, 230–237
Mohawk, 198
Morgan, Charley, 277
Morgan, Henry S., 84–86
Morgan, J. Pierpont, 7, 13, 47, 56, 67–75, 76
Morgan, J. Pierpont, Jr., 76–77, 84, 100, 152
Morgan family, 67–86, 89, 152
Morning Star, 210–212, 223, 226
Mosbacher, Bus, 260, 263, 264–271, 273

Namouna, 13
Nawanger, Maharaja of, 90
Nefertiti, 265, 299
Newmark, Steve and Esther, 184
Nina, 142, 145, 155, 193–207, 222
Nokomis, 94
North, Lowell, 300, 304
North Star, 5, 6, 47, 48–49, 89, 245
Nourmahal, 7, 14, 89, 90, 101, 176
Novak, Kim, 132
Noyes, Harry E., 212, 215
Noyes, Helen, 212

Oceanic, 75
Oceanographer, 80
Onassis, Aristotle, 128, 175
Ondine, 185
Oneida, 69
Onkahye, 30
Orion, 152
Osgood, George, 7, 68

Packer, Sir Frank, 277
Patria, 142, 143
Payne, Alan, 278
Pen Duick IV, 149
Perry, Townsend, 13
Persson, Seth, 232
Philadelphia, 271
Philante, 84
Phipps, Ogden, 175
Pierce, Henry Clay, 7–11, 67
Pinta, 145, 194, 197
Plant, Morgan, 215
Pluton, 71
Porter, William B., 76
Preble, Edward, 271
Priscilla, 113–114
Pulitzer, Joseph, 90

Rainbow, 62, 162, 164, 166, 168
Ranger, 62, 64, 65, 161–171, 175, 257
Rat of Wight, 1
Reliance, 164
Resolute, 144
Rhodes, Phil, 260
Rhodes, 236
Rigg, Bunny, 237
Robinson, John, 248
Roosevelt, Franklin Delano, 52, 101, 132
Root, Elihu, Jr., 194, 198
Rosenfeld, Stanley, 237
Rosenfeld, William, 237–238

Salmon, Paul, 281
Santa Maria, 194
Sappho, 215
Savarona II, 151–152
Savarona III, 151–155, 230
Schaefer, Rudolph, 44
Schuyler, George L., 30–31
Schwab, Charles S., 55
Sea Cloud, 127–134, 155, 230
Sentinel, 6
Shamrock, 62
Shenandoah II, 196
Slocum, Captain Joshua, 125
Somerset, Bobby, 199–200
Sopwith, T. O. M., 62, 84, 166–168
Southern Cross, 98–100, 298, 299
Sovereign, 263, 273, 292
Speejacks, 117

Star of India, 90
Steers, George, 31
Steers, James, 33, 36
Stephens, Olin J., 44–45, 65, 162, 166, 232, 238, 260, 263, 273, 277, 291
Stephens, Rod, 166
Stevens, Edward, 33
Stevens, Commodore John Cox, 29–45, 162
Still, Baxter, 222
Stormvogel, 204, 210, 226–227
Stormy Weather, 162, 216
Stranger, 7, 68
Strawbridge, William, 260
Sturrock, Jock, 269
Sunbeam, 5–6, 114
Sutton, George W., Jr., 94–97

Tabarly, Eric, 149
Tams, J. Frederick, 68–69
Tarantula, 56
Thistle, 139
Thomas, Patty, 252
Ticonderoga, 209–227
Tillie, 6
Tioga, 215–217
Titania, 44
Tod, Robert E., 139
Trujillo, Generalissimo Rafael, 127, 132, 134
Trujillo, Ramfils, 132, 134
Turner, Ted, 292–306

Vagrant, 47
Valfreya, 90
Valhalla, 139
Valiant, 277–278, 294
Vamarie, 216

Van Dyck, Steve, 276, 282, 283, 286, 287
Vanderbilt, Cornelius, 5, 47–49
Vanderbilt, Cornelius, II, 49
Vanderbilt, Cornelius, III, 49–55
Vanderbilt, Cornelius, IV, 52
Vanderbilt, Gertrude, 166
Vanderbilt, Gloria, 52
Vanderbilt, Harold S. "Mike," 47, 56, 62–65, 161–171, 260, 263, 274, 278
Vanderbilt, Reggie, 52
Vanderbilt, William Henry, 49
Vanderbilt, William Kissam, 49, 55
Vanderbilt, William Kissam, Jr., 56–62
Vanderbilt family, 47–65, 89, 101, 152, 161, 245
Vara, 165
Venturer, 238
Vergemere, 175
Victoria and Albert, 2, 5, 41
Vim, 65, 260, 274
Virginia, 59
Visser, Martin, 281–282, 283, 285, 286
Vogel, Dr. Karl, 116–117, 122–123
Volante, 39, 41
Voss, Captain John, 125

Wave, 29, 30
Weatherly, 260, 265, 277, 299
Wenner-Gren, Axel, 100
Williamsburgh, 175
Wilton, Earl of, 30, 36
Winchester, 47, 49–55
Windward Passage, 185

Yachting (magazine), 14, 94–97, 98, 131, 230
Yankee, 166–171